THE PRACTICAL U.S. RESOURCE GUIDE TO THE EUROPEAN UNION

THE PRACTICAL

U.S. RESOURCE GUIDE TO

THE EUROPEAN UNION

★ ★ ★

By Christian D. De Fouloy

★

KLUWER LAW INTERNATIONAL

The Hague • London • Boston

Published by Kluwer Law International,
P.O. Box 85889, 2508 CN The Hague, The Netherlands.

Sold and distributed in the U.S.A. and Canada
by Kluwer Law International,
675 Massachusetts Avenue, Cambridge, MA 02139, U.S.A.

In all other countries, sold and distributed
by Kluwer Law International,
P.O. Box 85889, 2508 CN The Hague, The Netherlands.

Although every effort has been made to make this Guide as accurate and comprehensive as possible, it cannot be regarded as all-inclusive and free from errors, nor does it purport to be authoritative as to legal status or relationship existing between the American firms and individuals involved and their business enterprises in Belgium. In no way shall the information sources herein referenced constitute any type of recommendation and/or endorsement. Furthermore, the author shall not be held liable for errors and/or omissions of whatever nature contained in this Guide. Readers are kindly invited to communicate eventual errors or omissions they may discover so further editions may be improved. The reproduction even partial by photo-mechanical process (photocopy, microscopy, scanner) as well as the reporting of addresses, nomenclature, etc. by word processor or any other means for professional, commercial or advertising purposes is forbidden.

LOBBY SOURCES EUROPE, 1998

ISBN 9041106413

CONTENTS

PART II
in the United States

ANNEXES

INTRODUCTION

Brussels is often compared to Washington DC in the sense that just as Washington DC is our Nation's Capital, Brussels is the seat of the Commission of the European Union and, hence, aims to be the Capital of Europe.

Public Affairs/Interest Representation is a key part of successful corporate strategy and, admittedly, it plays a big role in Brussels. An estimated 13,000 Public Affairs practitioners and 1,000 Journalists interact with over 30,000 Officials from the EU Institutions.

Brussels abounds with Consultants, Management Consultants, Public Affairs Advisors, Public Relations Agents, Regulatory Advocates (Lawyers), Lawyers and Corporate Representatives, Trade Federations and Associations, Trade Unions, Countries and Regions, and, increasingly, Public Interest Groups.

It is obvious that Americans have a vested interest in developing relations with the EU Institutions and more broadly in enhancing the understanding of policy-making and/or interests in the European environment.

The practice of Public Affairs is strongly influenced by the institutional, political, and social context in which it takes place. However, European diplomacy and methods of persuasion differ from the more open American approach, and European Public Affairs styles will continue to reflect these cultural and historical differences. In the United States, lobbying is institutionalized, regulated, entirely public and serves a recognized purpose, as part of a model of political balance between the Congress and the Administration. It should be noted, however, that the power to initiate legislation in the US lies with an elected body - Congress - and Members of Congress are open to quite different pressures from their counterparts in the European Commission. Powerful Interest Groups can exert pressure(s) on them through the contribution or withdrawal of electoral funds and through public relations campaigns, mobilizing public opinion in favor or against a particular point of view. As the European Parliament becomes more influential, however, and the legislative process in Europe becomes more democratic, the way in which that process is influenced by lobbyists may change.

While there is a strong American presence in Brussels, it is not easy, especially for the newcomer, to find his way around. There are plenty of Directories that are published about sources of information in the EU, but the material presented is for the most part geared to the Member States. Often, information of direct value for Americans is buried under a mountain of strictly EU sources of information. If the American Chamber of Commerce in Brussels is very active in Public Affairs and, an outstanding provider of EU information, it is by no means the only source of information that can be tapped. Recognition of the need for a more comprehensive survey of all available sources and contacts led to the development of this first US practical Guide to the EU.

This Guide aims to be a practical tool for Americans at home and abroad and all those who defend US interests throughout Europe to help them easily identify the services that can assist them, thus avoiding the maze of EU bureaucracy and wasted time.

For example, do you need an American lawyer specialized in EU matters? Easy, you refer to the legal section and you will have, at a glance, all American law firms represented in Brussels with the names of the Attorneys and their specialty. Do you want to contact the US Media? Easy, you refer to the appropriate media section and you will have the list of all US correspondents present in Brussels including the newspapers and/or magazines they represent and the issues they particularly follow. You need a Public Affairs Consultant in Brussels, and preferably you would like to locate a firm that has acquired experience in the representation of US interests and/or that has an affiliated office in the United States for ease of follow-up. Easy, you refer to the Consultants section and you will be able to make a selection based on facts. You are preparing a trip to Brussels and you would like to make appointments with key officials at the Commission or Parliament level, especially those that are responsible for relations with the USA. Easy, you refer to the appropriate sections and you will have the detailed listing of the key US expert people to contact with their address, telephone and fax numbers. And if you really want to feel at home, contact your state office either in Brussels or elsewhere in Europe. There are 30 states that have a European representation. Just turn to the appropriate section for the detailed listing of all US regional, city, state and port authorities on the Continent.

When I embarked upon the preparation of this Guide, my first and foremost objective was to provide a "one-source, American reference"; i.e. of "Americans serving Americans" in the Capital of Europe. I hope it is a good start in that direction.

To make this Guide even more valuable, it also offers sources of information on the European Union available on both sides of the Atlantic, it gives the University Libraries in the US that maintain publications dealing with the EU and the list of lecturers/experts throughout the US, who, upon request, can deliver presentations about the EU on the occasion of conferences, seminars, meetings, etc..

USE AND ORGANIZATION OF THIS GUIDE

This US Guide to the EU is more than just a list of people and organizations. Whenever possible, we have provided detailed descriptions about the activities that are carried out.

This Guide is divided into two (2) Parts :

- **Part I** is divided into 16 Chapters, and focuses on all US sources of information to the EU in Brussels, the capital of Europe and of European Public Affairs. Here is an overview of their content.

  - *Chapter 1* - US Mission to the EU. The US Diplomatic Representation to the European Union.

  - *Chapter 2* - The American Chamber of Commerce. The American Chamber of Commerce in Brussels plays an active role in the area of Public Affairs, primarily through the EU-Committee.

  - *Chapter 3* - The American-European Community Association (ACEA). A prestigious, independent, non-partisan, non-profit organization providing a strategic platform for discussion of political and economic issues between the US and the EU at the highest level.

  - *Chapter 4* - The Transatlantic Business Dialogue (TABD). Launched in 1995, the aim of the TABD is to boost transatlantic trade and investment opportunities through the removal of costly inefficiencies caused by excessive regulation, duplication and differences in the EU and US regulatory systems and procedures.

  - *Chapter 5* - Key people dealing with the USA at the European Commission level, including listing by Directorate General.

  - *Chapter 6* - Key people dealing with the USA at the European Parliament level, including Parliamentary Committee and Delegation.

  - *Chapter 7* - US Trade Associations represented in Brussels on behalf of specific US or industrial sectors at the European level. Their main purpose is usually to assure a liaison with the European Union Institutions and to inform their members of developments of interest.

  - *Chapter 8* - US Regional, City, State, Port Authorities Representations. A comprehensive listing not just limited to Brussels but to all of Europe by country and by city.

- *Chapter 9* - US Consultants specializing in EU matters. They are primarily Political, Economic and Management Consultants specializing in EU Affairs.

- *Chapter 10* - Other Consultants specializing in EU matters. They are listed because they have Affiliates and/or Correspondent Offices in the USA.

- *Chapter 11* - US Law Firms represented in Brussels. Lists firms specializing in European Law and/or European Affairs. They are listed alphabetically providing US HQ, Brussels address, names of Attorneys, number of Attorneys specializing in EU Law and their prime areas of concentration.

- *Chapter 12* - US Banks represented in Brussels.

- *Chapter 13* - US Accounting Firms represented in Brussels.

- *Chapter 14* - US Media and newspapers represented in Brussels including alphabetical listing of US Journalists and Press Agencies reporting from Brussels on Europe and their specialty.

- *Chapter 15* - Major US Corporate Representations to the EU. Alphabetical listing of major US Corporations maintaining full-time European Affairs Directors or other Executives with other titles who deal in EU Government Affairs.

- *Chapter 16* - The American Club of Brussels (ACB)

- **Part II** is divided into 3 Chapters and focuses on all EU sources of information in the United States.

    - *Chapter 1* - EU Delegation to the US, Office of Press and Public Affairs, EU Delegation to the United Nations, EU/US Chamber of Commerce, European Document Research, Electronic Information Products Distributors.

    - *Chapter 2* - Team Europe Information Service. Network of EU/Lecturers/Experts in the United States. Alphabetical and Geographical Listing.

    - *Chapter 3* - EU-Information Centers in the USA. Alphabetical Listing of US Universities that are recipients of all EU Publications.

PART I

In Brussels, Belgium

CHAPTER 1
US MISSION TO THE EU

United States Mission to the European Union
Boulevard du Régent, 40
B-1000 Brussels
Tel : (32) (2) 508-2222 Fax : (32) (2) 511-2092
HE A. Vernon-Weaver, Head of Mission Tel : (32) (2) 508-2750
Donald B. Kursch, Deputy Head of Mission Tel : (32) (2) 508-2752

The US Mission to the EU represents a precious source of information for American companies and/or trade organizations. Counsellors at the US Mission keep fully abreast of all developments in the trade, technical, financial and cultural areas between the US and the EU. The US Mission includes the following sections :

AGRICULTURE
(Vacant), Minister Counselor
Bobby G. Richey, Senior Agricultural Attaché
James W. Johnson, Agricultural Officer
Ralph Gifford, Agricultural Officer
Gerda Vandercammen, Agricultural Specialist
Alex Thiermann, APHIS Regional Director
Nicholas Gutierrez, Assistant Regional Director

COMMERCIAL AFFAIRS
(Vacant), Minister Counselor
Stewart Ballard, Commercial Attaché
Helen Davis Delaney, Standards Officer
Orri Hlodversson, Commercial Specialist
Eric Fleury, Seafood Industry Specialist
Sylvia Mohr, Commercial Assistant

CUSTOMS AFFAIRS
Robert Mall, Customs Attaché
James Petree, Customs Representative
Jacqueline Herzog, Program Assistant

ECONOMIC AFFAIRS
Michael Gallagher, Minister Counselor
Noney Adams, Trade Policy Attaché
Hanneke Siebelink, Economic Analyst

GENERAL ECONOMIC POLICY UNIT
David Burnett, Chief
Howard D. Clark, Industry Policy Officer
Amy Westling, Intellectual Property & Services Officer

ENVIRONMENT, SCIENCE, TECHNOLOGY & ENERGY
Colin Helmer, Chief Tel : (32)(2) 508-2781
Kenneth H. Merten, Environment Officer
Bartholomew Barbessi, Science & Technology Officer

OFFICE OF THE TREASURY REPRESENTATIVE
Gregory Berger, Financial Attaché Tel : (32)(2) 508-2668

POLITICAL AFFAIRS
Todd Becker, Political Counselor
James Glenn, Labor Counselor

THIRD PILLAR UNIT
Brian R. Stickney, Counsellor
Laurier Mailloux, US AID Representative
Drew Arena, Justice Representative

EXTERNAL AFFAIRS DIVISION
Sharon White, Coordinator
Richard Figueroa, External Affairs Officer
Bill Regan, External Affairs Officer

INSTITUTIONAL AFFAIRS DIVISION
William E. Lucas, Coordinator
Nan Kennelly, Population, Refugee & Migration Officer
Roland Deglain, Political Specialist

PRESS & PUBLIC AFFAIRS
Veda Wilson, Public Affairs Counselor
Benedict Duffy, Deputy Counselor
Elizabeth Cramaussel, Cultural Affairs Assistant
Gery Jacobs, Senior Information Assistant
(Vacant), Information Assistant

UNITED STATES MISSION TO THE EUROPEAN UNION

Driver
Paul Lunts

Protocol Assistant
Magali Mizon

Special Assistant
Page Atkins

Secretary
Catherine Allen

Secretary
Linda Ingalls

EMBASSOR

DE MISSION

Administrative Assistant
Danny Hansgrove

Administrative Clerk
Oliver De Murphy

Driver/Admin support
Alain Dupuis

Commercial Attache
Stewart Ballard

Standards Officer
Helen Delaney

Commercial Specialist
Orn Hindrewssson

Seafood Industry Specialist
Eric Flowry

Commercial Assistant
Sylvia Mohr

Administrative Assistant
Veronique Sundsten

Standards Assistant
Carol Provoa

EC Tender Reporter
Doris Ling

Program Assistant
Pauline Clark

Program Assistant
Monique Derphox

Program Assistant
Linda Nield

Secretary
Patricia Vliax

Labor & Deputy Political Counselor
James H. Gideon

External Affairs Unit

External Affairs Coordinator
Sharon White

Secretary
Debbie Barbezei

External Affairs Officer
Richard Figueroa

External Affairs Officer
William Regan

Institutional Affairs Unit

Institutional Affairs Coordinator
William Lucas

Institutional Affairs Officer
Vacant

Political Specialist
Rolana Dygtan

Economic Specialist
Hannele Sielelimi

Secretary
David Weinberg

Customs Representative
Mark Lura

Technical Attache
Harry Waskewicz

Technical Attache
Neil Leigh

Secretary
Jacqueline Herzog

Secretary
Barrie Resoloff

Environment, Science, Technology & Energy Unit Chief
Colin Helmer

Secretary
Patricia Houston

Environment & Trade Officer
Kenneth H. Mervn

Environment & Fisheries Officer
Bartholomew Barbezei

General Economic Policy Unit Chief
David Barmen

Secretary
Vacant

Industry Policy Officer
Howard D. Clark

Intellectual Property & Services Officer
Amy Wedding

Deputy PAC
Ben Duffy

Cultural Affairs Assistant
Elisabeth Crumaccuel

Senior Information Assistant
Gerry Jacobs

Information Assistant
Caroline Hommec

Administrative Assistant
Ann Smith

Secretary
Gene Verbist

Senior Ag. Attache
Bobby Richey

Agricultural Officer
Ralph Gifford

Agricultural Officer
James W. Johnson

Agricultural Specialist
Gerda Vanderkrummen

Agricultural Specialist
Danielle Boeremans

FAS Secy-Office Mngr.
Kathy Larkin-Soane

Agricultural Clerk
Hilde Braun

Contract Secretary
Melissa Ash

Assistant Regional Director (Plant Health Attache)
Nicholas Contreez

Secretary
Belinda Joerden

Layout: ADMIN/NH/hansgrove/November 1997

DIPLOMATIC CORPS ACCREDITED
TO THE EUROPEAN UNION

There are 165 countries (beside the 15 member states) that maintain a Mission to the European Union.

AFGHANISTAN
ALBANIA
ALGERIA
ANDORRA (Principality)
ANGOLA
ANTIGUA & BARBUDA
ARGENTINA
ARMENIA
AUSTRALIA
AZERBAIJAN
BAHAMAS
BANGLADESH
BARBADOS
BELARUS
BELIZ
BENIN
BHUTAN
BOLIVIA
BOTSWANA
BOSNIA-HERZEGOVINA
BRAZIL
BRUNEI
BULGARIA
BURKINA FASO
BURUNDI
CAMBODIA
CAMEROON
CANADA
CAPE VERDE
CARIBBEAN (East)
CENTRAFRICAN REPUBLIC
CHAD
CHILE
CHINA (People's Republic)
COLOMBIA

COMORO ISLANDS
CONGO
CONGO (Rep. Dem.)
COSTA RICA
CROATIA
CUBA
CYPRUS
CZECH REPUBLIC
DJIBOUTI
DOMINICAN REPUBLIC
DOMINICA
ECUADOR
EGYPT
EL SALVADOR
EQUATORIAL GUINEA
ERITREA
ESTONIA
ETHIOPIA
FIJI
GABON
GAMBIA
GEORGIA
GHANA
GRENADA
GUATEMALA
GUINEA
GUINEA BISSAU
GUYANA
HAITI
HOLY SEE
HONDURAS
HONG KONG
HUNGARY
ICELAND
INDIA

INDONESIA	NORWAY
IRAQ	OMAN
IRAN	PAKISTAN
IVORY COAST	PANAMA
JAMAICA	PAPUA NEW GUINEA
JAPAN	PARAGUAY
JORDAN	PERU
KAZAKHSTAN	PHILIPPINES
KENYA	POLAND
KIRGHIZIA	QATAR
KOREA (South)	ROMANIA
KUWAIT	RUSSIA (Federation)
LAOS	RWANDA
LATVIA	SOLOMON ISLANDS
LESOTHO	SAO TOME E PRINCIPE
LEBANON	SAUDI ARABIA
LIBERIA	SENEGAL
LIBYA	SEYCHELLES
LIECHTENSTEIN	SIERRA LEONE
LITHUANIA	SINGAPORE
MACAO	SLOVAKIA
MADAGASCAR	SLOVENIA
MALAYSIA	SRI-LANKA
MALAWI	ST CHRISTOPHER & NEVIS
MALDIVES	ST VINCENT & GRENADINES
MALI	SUDAN
MALTA	SURINAM
MOROCCO	SWAZILAND
MAURITANIA	SWITZERLAND
MAURITIUS	SYRIA
MEXICO	TANZANIA
MOLDOVIA	THAILAND
MONGOLIA	TOGO
MONTSERRAT	TONGA
MOZAMBIQUE	TRINIDAD & TOBAGO
NYANMAR	TUNISIA
NAMIBIA	TURKEY
NEPAL	UKRAINE
NEW ZEALAND	UNITED STATES OF AMERICA
NICARAGUA	URUGUAY
NIGER	UZBEKISTAN
NIGERIA	VENEZUELA

VIETNAM
WESTERN SAMOA
YEMEN (Republic)

YUGOSLAVIA
ZAMBIA
ZIMBABWE

CHAPTER 2
AMERICAN CHAMBER OF COMMERCE

EU-COMMITTEE
Avenue des Arts 50, Bte 5
B-1000 Brussels
Tel : (32) (2) 513-6770
Fax : (32) (2) 513-3590
Mr John Russel , Director of Public Affairs
Tel : (32) (2) 513-6892

The Chamber serves as a spokeperson to Belgian, EU and US government authorities, and offers constructive input over a wide range of issues, in which it has particular expertise.

The EU-Committee of the Chamber plays an important role in EU Affairs. The EU-Committee has expanded its membership from 40 in 1985 to 143 in 1997. Its members are drawn from the highest ranks of US industry, including 9 of Fortune's Top 10 US industrial corporations. The EU-Committee speaks for the European Council of American Chambers of Commerce (ECAC), an Association of 14 American Chambers throughout Europe, representing 20,000 companies, 200 billion dollars of US investment in Europe and 10 million European employees.

The EU-Committee's own member companies are, of course, responsible for employing a significant portion of that number, which gives the Committee's views particular weight with the Community institutions. EU Lawyers and Consultants are also members, although their membership is restricted to 25% of the total to ensure that the EU-Committee retains its original bias towards industry. There is currently a 4 year waiting list for EU Lawyers and Consultants.

The rapid growth in the membership of the EU-Committee has taken place principally in the last 3 years, reflecting the reputation of the Committee as an effective lobbying organization and the growing interest of US companies in EU legislation.

While the EU-Committee does not have a direct consultative status, it is represented on the European Commission's Services Group, and is frequently invited to participate in Working Groups or to attend them with observer status.

In short, The EU-Committee seeks to represent in an effective and timely manner the views of European companies of American parentage to the European Institutions and to National Governments on European policy and legislative initiatives of concern to business operating in Europe. The EU-Committee seeks to raise awareness of the economic, technological and social contributions made by its member companies in Europe and of their commitment to the achievement of European integration.

From an organizational standpoint, the EU-Committee is comprised of one (1) Chairman and two (2) Senior Vice-Chairmen :

CHAIR :
Mr William Seddon-Brown, Director European Government Affairs
Waste Management Int. Services Ltd.
Avenue de Tervueren 13
B-1040 Brussels
Tel : (32) (2) 732-3935
Fax : (32) (2) 732-6825

Senior Vice-Chairmen :
Mr Jan Candries, Director European Affairs
Ford of Europe, Inc.
Boulevard de la Woluwe 2
B-1150 Brussels
Tel : (32) (2) 762-1070
Fax : (32) (2) 762-9564

Ms Maria Laptev, European Affairs Director
Charles Barker Plc
Rue Montoyer 31, Bte 2
B-1000 Brussels
Tel : (32) (2) 511-0645
Webside : http://www.charker.co.uk
Email : marial@charker.co.uk
Fax : (32) (2) 512-5344

The EU Committee is broken down into 13 Subcommittees, made up of about 50-60 company Representatives and Specialists , who meet on a monthly basis to discuss crucial issues and work out Position Papers. In addition, some Task-Forces are set up to deal with issues requiring particular attention : The 13 Subcommittees are :

1. Communications,
2. Competition Policy,
3. Consumer Affairs,
4. Environmental Health and Safety,
5. Financial Services and Company Law,
6. Fiscal Initiative,
7. Industrial Affairs,
8. Institutional Affairs,
9. Intellectual Property,
10. Social Affairs,
11. Telecommunications,
12. Trade & External Affairs
13. Transportation.

1. Communications

Chair :
Mr John Candries, Director European Affairs
Ford of Europe, Inc.
Boulevard de la Woluwe 2
B-1150 Brussels
Tel : (32) (2) 762-1070
Fax : (32) (2) 762-9564

This Subcommittee concentrates its particular attention on the EU Directorate General X (DG X) " Information, Communication, Culture and Audiovisual ", including :

- Directorate A : Central Information Office
- Directorate B : Information Networks
- Directorate C : Audiovisual Policy, Culture and Sport
- Directorate D : Communication

2. Competition policy

Chair :
Mr Izzet M. Sinan, Counsel
Morogon, Lewis & Bockius LLP
Counsellors at Law
Rue Guimard 7
B-1040 Brussels

Tel : (32) (2) 512-5501
Fax : (32) (2) 512-5889

This Subcommittee concentrates is particular attention on the EU Directorate General (IX) (DG IV) " Competition ", including :

- Directorate A : General Competition Policy and Coordination
- Directorate B : Merger Task Force
- Directorate C : Information, Communication and Multimedia
- Directorate D : Services
- Directorate E : Basic Industries and Energy
- Directorate F : Capital and Consumer Goods Industries
- Directorate G : State Aids

3. Consumer Affairs

Chair :
Ms Susan England
Ernst & Young Europe
Avenue Marcel Thiry 204
B-1200 Brussels
Tel : (32) (2) 774-9111
Fax : (32) (2) 774-9090

This Subcommittee concentrates its particular attention on the EU Directorate General XXIV (DG XXIV) " Consumer Policy and Consumer Health Protection", including :

- Directorate A : Community Actions in Consumers' Interest

4. Environmental Health & Safety

Chair :
Ms Margareth M. O'Donnell, EU Liaison
Pennzoil Company
Place du Tomberg, 8
B-1200 Brussels
Tel : (32) (2) 779-2015
Email : 100446.1400@compuserve.com
Fax : (32) (2) 773-9302

This Subcommittee concentrates its particular attention on the EU Directorate General XI (DG XI) " Environment, Nuclear Safety and Civil Protection ", including :

- Directorate A : General and International Matters
- Directorate B : Environmental Instruments
- Directorate C : Nuclear Security and Civil Protection
- Directorate D : Environment Quality and Natural Resources
- Directorate E : Industry and Environment

5. Financial Services and Company Law

Chair :
Mr Thomas Huertas
Citibank Boulevard Général Jacques 263 g
B-1050 Brussels
Tel : (32) (2) 626-5111
Webside : http://www.citibank.com
Fax : (32) (2) 626-5584

This Subcommittee concentrates its particular attention on the EU Directorate General XV (DG XV) " Internal Market and Financial Services ", including :

- Directorate A : General Matters and Coordination;
  Free Movement of Persons and Direct Taxation
- Directorate B : Free Movement of Goods and
  Public Procurement
- Directorate C : Financial Institutions
- Directorate D: Free Movement of Information, Company Law
  and Financial Information

6.Fiscal Initiatives

Chair :
Mr Patrick Kelley
Boden , De Bandt, De Braux, Jeantet, Lagerlöf & Uria
Rue Brederode 13 A
B-1000 Brussels
Tel : (32) (2) 505-0211
Fax : (32) (2) 502-2644

NOTES :

The Firm of Boden, De Bandt, De Brauw, Jeantet, Lagerlöf & Uria is not an American Law Firm but an Alliance of European Lawyers.

This Subcommittee concentrates its particular attention on Directorate General XV (DG XV) " Internal Market and Financial Services ", including:

- Directorate A : Direct Taxation as well as on Directorate General XXI (DG XXI) " Customs and Indirect Taxation " including :
- Directorate C : Indirect Taxation

7. Industrial Affairs

Chair :
Ms Lizanne Scott
Digital Equipment Corporation
Rue de l' Aéronef, 1
B-1140 Brussels
Tel : (32) (2) 729-7111
Fax : (32) (2) 726-4560

This Subcommittee concentrates its particular attention on EU Directorate General III (DG III) " Industry ", including

- Directorate A : Industrial Policy
- Directorate B : Legislation and Standardization and Telematics Networks
- Directorate C : Industrial Affairs I : Basic Industries
- Directorate D : Industrial Affairs II : Capital Goods Industries
- Directorate E : Industrial Affairs III : Consumer Goods Industries
- Directorate F : Research &Technological Development (R&TD) : Information Technology

8. Institutional Affairs

Chair :
Mr Stanley Crossick
European Policy Center
Boulevard Charlemagne 42
B-1040 Brussels
Tel : (32) (2) 231-0340
Fax : (32) (2) 231-0704

This Subcommittee concentrates its particular attention on the Secretariat General of the EU Commission, namely :

- Directorate B : Coordination I : Institutional Matters;
  Community Law;
  Information Technology; Publications

NOTE :

Institutional issues fall directly under the responsability of the President of the European Commission (Mr Jacques Santer)

9. Intellectual Property

Chair :
Mr Cees Van Rij
Oppenheimer, Wolff & Donelly
Avenue Louise 240
B-1050 Brussels
Tel : (32) (2) 626-0500
Webside : http://www.owdlaw.com
Email : eosterweil@owdlaw.com
Fax : (32) (2) 626-0510

This Subcommittee concentrates its particular attention on EU Directorate General (IV) (DG IV) " Competition ", namely :

- Directorate C : Information, Communication and Multimedia
  (Aspects of Intellectual Property)

Directorate General I (DG I) " External Relations : Commercial Policy, Relation with North America ", namely :

- Directorate D : "Sectoral Commercial Questions, Market Access" (New technologies, Intellectual Property and Public Procurement)

Directorate General XIII (DG XIII) " Telecommunications, Information Market and Exploitation of Research ", namely :

- Directorate D : Research and Technological Development (R &TD) : Dissemination and Exploitation of R &TD Results, Technology Transfer and Innovation (Strategic Aspects of Innovation and Exploitation of Research and Technological Development, and Intellectual Property)

Directorate General XV (DG XV) " Internal Market and Financial Services ", namely :

- Directorate E : Intellectual and Industrial Property, Freedom of Establishment and Freedom to Provide Services, notably in the Regulated Professions, the Media (Industrial Property, including International Aspects / Copyright and Neighboring Rights, including International Aspects / The Media, Commercial Communication and Unfair Competition)

10. Social Affairs

Chair :
Mr Philip Cappuyns
Exxon Company International
Boulevard du Souverain 280
B-1160 Brussels
Tel : (32) (2) 674-4111
Fax : (32) (2) 674-4129

This Subcommittee concentrates its particular attention on EU Directorate General (V) (DG V) " Employment, Industrial Relations and Social Affairs), including :

- Directorate A : Employment and Labour Market
- Directorate B : European Social Fund : Policy Development
- Directorate C : European Social Fund : Operation

- Directorate D : Social Dialogue and Freedom of Movement
for Workers
- Directorate E : Social Policy and Action
- Directorate F : Public Health and Safety at Work

11. Telecommunications

Chair :
Ms Karen Corbett-Sanders, Regional Director, Government Affairs
Nynex
Research Park Kranenberg 6
B-1731 Zellik
Tel : (32) (2) 463-3201
Fax : (32) (2) 463-1706

This Subcommittee concentrates its particular attention on EU Directorate General XIII (DG XIII) " Telecommunications, Information Market and Exploitation of Research ", namely :

- Directorate A : Telecommunications, Transeuropean Networks
and Services, Postal Services
- Directorate B : Advanced Communications Technologies
and Services
- Directorate C : Telematics Applications (Networks
and Services)
- Directorate D : Research and Technological Development
(R&TD) : Dissemination and Exploitation
of R&TD Results,
Technology Transfer and Innovation
- Directorate E : Information Industry and Market and
Language Processing

12. Trade and External Affairs

Chair :
Mr James Lockett
Allied Signal Europe SA
Haasrode Research Park
Grauwmeer 1
B-3001 Leuven

Tel : (32) (16) 39 13 00
Fax : (32) (16) 40 08 74

This Subcommittee concentrates its particular attention on EU Directorate General I (DG I) " External Relations : Commercial Policy and Relations with North America, the Far East, Australia and New Zealand ", namely :

- Directorate B : Relations with North America, Australia, New Zealand, NAFTA and APEC
- Directorate C: Anti-Dumping Strategy : Dumping Aspects (Policy, Investigations and Measures)
- Directorate D : Sectorial Commercial Questions, Market Access
- Directorate E : Anti-Dumping Strategy : Injury and Community Interest Aspects (Policy, Investigations and Measures); Other Instruments of External Economic Policy and General Questions
- Directorate F : Relations with Far Eastern Countries
- Directorate G : WTO, OECD, Commercial Questions with Respect to Agriculture and Fisheries; Export Credit Policy
- Directorate M : Services and External dimension of the Union; External Relations in the Research, Science, Nuclear Energy and Environment Fields

13. Transportation

Chair :
Mr Anton Van der Lande
United Parcel Services
Woluwelaan 158
B-1831 Diegem
Tel : (32) (2) 706-2807
Fax : (32) (2) 247-2940

This Subcommittee concentrates is particular attention on EU Directorate General VII (DG II) " Transport ", namely :

- Directorate A : International Relations and Trans-European Transport and Infrastructure Networks
- Directorate B : Inland Transport

- Directorate C : Air Transport
- Directorate D : Maritime Transport
- Directorate E : Development of Transport Policy and Research and Development

STRENGTHS OF THE EU-COMMITTEE

The EU-COMMITTEE

The EU-Committee prides itself on :

- Recognizing an emerging issue and getting a Position Paper rapidly (It takes between 6 to 8 weeks to draft a Position Paper),
- Producing high quality Position Papers, both in terms of content and style.
- Using a constructive approach. The EU-Committee is never negative about the Commission's Proposals. It addresses the Commission's Proposals Article by Article, Line by Line, suggesting language and definitional changes, which the Commission staff or the European Parliament find very useful to their work.

In conclusion, the EU-Committee's contributions are always well received by the Commission even though it represents US rather than European companies' interests.

Before closing this Chapter on the Amcham/EU-Committee, mention should be made of the European-American Industrial Council (EAIC), whose Secretariat support is located at the EU-Committee of Amcham. Established in 1993, EAIC is comprised of a grouping of 25 Senior Executives from among the largest multinational companies throughout Europe of US parentage. EAIC provides an opportunity for networking and discussing public policy issues of mutual interest and concern to member corporations, that translates into recommendations and dialogue with Officials of the European institutions. A Steering Group, comprised of the Chair and Vice-Chair meets three times a year to prepare and set the Agenda for the plenary sessions.

For further information, Contact :

European-American Industrial Council - (EAIC)
Secretariat

The U.S. Practical Guide
to the European Union

Avenue des Arts 50, Bte 5
B-1000 Brussels
Tel : (32) (2) 513-6892
Fax : (32) (2) 513-7928
E-mail : eaic@post 1.amcham.be
Franco Mariotti (Hewlett Packard), Chairman
Juergen Aumueller (American Express), Vice-Chairman
Vito Baumgartner (Caterpillar), Vice-Chairman
Chiara Scimemi, EAIC,Manager

CHAPTER 3
THE AMERICAN EUROPEAN COMMUNITY
ASSOCIATION (AECA)

THE AMERICAN EUROPEAN COMMUNITY ASSOCIATION (AECA)
Avenue de Messidorlaan 208, Bte 1
B-1180 Brussels
Tel : (32) (2) 344-5949
Fax : (32) (2) 344-5343
Sir David Nicolson, Founder & International Chairman
Baron Jacques Groothaert, Chairman
Mr Lucien R. Lelièvre, Founder and Honorary Director General
Mr Georges H. de Veirman, Director General and CEO
Ms Ann Roberts, Executive Director

Independent Non-partisan, Non-profit Association providing a strategic platform where business leaders from North America and Europe, together with members of the US Congress and US Officials, can informally discuss political and economic issues.

Mission / Aims :

• Providing a Forum for European and Transatlantic dialogue
• Stimulating mutual understanding and cooperation within Europe and between Europe and North America.
• Strengthening the European Transatlantic links between leading businessmen, politicians, officials and academicians
• Facilitating high level informal contact group
• Encouraging the initiation and stimulation of opportunities in Europe and across the Atlantic

Participants

Senior Executives from :

- Business, Industry and Services in three main target groups :
    - 1. Chairmen, Presidents, CEOs
    - 2. General Managers, Managing Directors
    - 3. Public Affairs & Government Affairs Directors
- European Union : Commission, Council, Parliament, European Investment Bank (EIB), European Bank for Reconstruction Development (EBRD) etc.,
- United States and NAFTA : Government, Departments, Congress, etc.,
- International Institutions : NATO, Council of Europe, United Nations Organizations (UNO), International Monetary Fund (IMF), College of Europe, World Trade Organization (WTO)
- Politics, Sciences, Academia, Media

Activity Objectives :

- Themes : Current issues - economics, business, trade, political, cultural, social, concerning cooperation within Europe and between North America and Europe.
- Conferences, symposia, receptions, exchange visits, etc
- Balanced selection of participants at activities by target group
- Cooperation within AECA Chapters in Europe and North America
- Meetings organized in cooperation with European and North America with :
    - Business and Government leaders,
    - Legislators and Officials from Federal & State / Regional Levels,
    - Embassies and States / Regional Representations

CHAPTER 4
THE TRANSATLANTIC BUSINESS
DIALOGUE (TABD)

The Objective

The aim of the Transatlantic Business Dialogue is to boost Transatlantic trade and investment oppportunities through the removal of costly inefficiencies caused by excessive regulations, duplication and differences in the EU and US regulatory systems and procedures.

The Origins

The TABD was launched in Seville, Spain in November 1995 at a Conference attended by CEOs from more than 100 US and EU companies and by top government representatives led by European Commissioners for Trade and Industry, and by the US Secretary of Commerce.

The New Transatlantic Marketplace

The creation of a new transatlantic marketplace permitting goods, services and capital to flow more easily across the Atlantic requires the progressive removal of traditional transatlantic trade and investment barriers and a convergence of national laws and regulations. This will improve trade and investment conditions, accelerate growth, create jobs and improve competitiveness.

By trading more efficiently across the Atlantic, the EU and US face the challenge of the global marketplace from a more competitive position, which will also act as a catalyst to increased trade and investment worldwide.

The EU-US relationship.

The importance of the transatlantic marketplace is underlined by the magnitude of the EU - US trading relationship - the biggest in the world.

In 1996 two-way trade in goods and services amounted to US $ 366 billion.

The EU currently accounts for 58 % of total foreign direct investment in the US while 44 % of US foreign direct investment is located in the EU. On each side of the Atlantic, more than 3 million jobs depend on these investments.

The strenghtening of EU - US economic relations should be seen within the context of worldwide multilateral cooperation.

The TABD fully supports the rules and principles of the World Trade Organization (WTO) and recognizes the need for any bilateral or plurilateral agreements to be WTO compatible.

An Effective Process - Not an Organization

The TABD is a unique process, driven by business leaders. It is unique because of the personal involvement of CEOs working closely with the highest levels of government from the EU and the US.

It is not an organization, but an effective framework for enhanced cooperation between business and governments, drawing on the expertise of existing organizations already working in the area of transatlantic relations.

This TABD is designed to deliver joint industry messages much faster than traditional methods of working with governments.

It allows direct industry input into government-to-government negotiating processes, by using the strength of consensus between EU and US business.

Both the US Government and the European Commission have made commitments to pursue TABD recommendations and are working actively to implement them.

The results which this unprecedented approach can deliver were demonstrated at the Chicago Conference in November 1996, when progress was achieved on a number of issues which will deliver advantages to consumers and companies alike.

The working method

The TABD is co-chaired by two senior business executives, one from the EU, one from the US. In 1996, the Chairmen were Jurgen Strube (BASF) and Alex Trotman (Ford).

Chairing the process in 1997 are, for the US side, Dana Mead, CEO Tenneco and Jan Timmer, Former CEO of Philips Electronics.

At the working level a Steering Committee brings together " issue managers " and representatives of the US Governement, the European Commission and the EU Presidency.

Many companies are contributing expertise and resources to the process, working together with major representative business organizations

Joint EU - US Issue Groups have been set up to make recommendations on key priorities for the transatlantic business community. Each group is led by an Issue Manager, one in the US, one in the EU. They are the focal point for input; they mobilize suppport from business and government; they seek concensus and prepare joint recommendations for concrete action against obstacles to trade and investment; they encourage progress and work with governments to achieve tangible results.

CEO - Level Conference

In addition to on-going activity at the working level, a conference is held each year to bring together CEOs and senior-level government representatives, to measure progress, discuss problem areas and develop new initiatives.

The unique combination of CEOs and Senior Government Representatives provides an unprecedented opportunity to achieve breakthroughs on challenging issues.

The Scope of the TABD

At the working level the TABD has so far more than 15 focused groups. They have been gathered together into 4 clusters under the active leadership of designated CEOs.

This format is designated to ensure effective coordination, raise visibility and maximize results.

Transatlantic Advisory Committee on Standards (TACS)

The TACS is driving towards a new regulatory model based on the principle " approved once, accepted everywhere ", on both sides of the Atlantic. It is developing detailed action plans to remove obstacles associated with Standards, Testing and Certification. It approaches this in two ways : the first is by targeting specific horizontal issues such as Mutual Recognition, Conformity Assessment and Greater Use of International Standards; the second is by targeting issues of special importance to individual sectors. So far more than 15 sectors have actively participated in this group, which has already produced tangible results.

Business Facilitation

This cluster brings together groups focused on convergence of policies in important areas for transatlantic trade. Their objective is ensuring the smooth operation of the new transatlantic marketplace; and is concerned with seeing progress in the following subjects : Taxation, Export Controls, Foreign Policy Measures, Customs, Product Liability, Electronic Commerce, Accountancy Standards and International Business Practices.

Global issues

This cluster brings together groups seeking to promote development of the global trading system through joint actions to stimulate and strengthen the multilateral trading framework. It pays special attention to issues which are primarily relevant to the operation of the new transatlantic marketplace within the context of global trading system.

These include WTO issues in general, the Information Technology Agreement, Financial Services, Government Procurement, Intellectual Property, Investment and Competition.

Small and Medium Sized Enterprises (SMEs)

The objective of this group is promoting transatlantic links between small and medium-sized businesses. It focuses on initiatives to stimulate the growth of SMEs which make a significant contribution to the economies of the EU and the US.

Selected TABD Areas of Focus

1. Standards, Certification and Regulatory Policy

- Mutual Recognition of International Harmonization of Product and Process Standards or Regulations.
- Testing and certification in various manufacturing sectors (Agri-biotech, Automotive, Chemicals, Cosmetics, Dietary Supplements, Electrical, Electronics, Heavy Equipment, Information Technology, Medical Devices, Pharmaceuticals, Recreational Marine, Telecommunications, Tires and Toys)
- Conformity Assessment and Labelling requirements.

2. Business facilitation

- Taxation
- Export Controls and Foreign Policy Measures
- Customs
- Product Liability
- Environmental Business Practices
- Electronic Commerce
- Accountancy Standards

3. Global issues

- WTO issues
- Financial Services
- Information Technology Agreements
- Government Procurement
- Intellectual Property
- Investment
- Compensation

TABD (Trans Atlantic Business Dialogue) Key Contacts

US

Mr Dona Mead, CEO Tenneco - 1997 TABD US Chair
Mr Ted Austell III, Tenneco - US Chairman of TABD Steering Committee
Tel : (1) (202) 942-0238
Fax : (1) (202) 638-3306

US SME Issue Manager - (Small Business Initiative)
Mr Mark Struhs, Vice President Sales/Marketing
Dynamo Ltd
Tel : (1) (817) 284-0114 x 202
Fax : (1) (817) 284-7606

EU

Mr Jan Timmer Former CEO Philips - 1997 TABD EU Chair
Mr Craig Burchell, Philips Electronics - EU Chairman of TABD Steering Committee
Tel : (32) (2) 231-1728
Fax : (32) (2) 231-0254

European SME Issue Manager - (Small Business Initiative)
Mr Jean Heymans, Secretary General
CECIMO (European Committee for Cooperation of the Machine Tool Industries)
Avenue Louise 66 B
B-1050 Brussels
Tel : (32) (2) 502-7090
Fax : (32) (2) 502-6082

Example of Transatlantic Small Business Initiative

In November 1996, the Transatlantic Small Business Initiative (TASBI) was launched by the European Commission and the US Department of Commerce to facilitate cooperation, trade and investment flows between European and American Small and Medium Sized Enterprises (SMEs). TASBI organizes sectoral partnering events in order to stimulate commercial alliances and exchanges of technological expertise, and is developing data resources to help SMEs identify business partners and research the trading environment in the United States.

Concrete Example :

In 1996, 118 European automotive industry enterprises and organizations went to SAE 96. (Society of Automotive Engineers Expo in Detroit, Michigan). In 1997, 141 European automotive suppliers and trade bodies made the trip, supported and co-ordinated by Directorate General XXIII (DG XXIII). They exhibited in a European village and took part in a number of highly effective meetings with matched US counterparts. A Sales and Marketing Director of a US car components manufacturer reported that the pre-arranged meetings were his most productive in 20 years of visiting the SAE Fair.

The US company will pursue links with companies in Spain, Germany and the UK, and is already discussing possibility of joint work with an Italian company. On the European side, one Italian company is in the process of establishing a Michigan office, a direct result of contacts made at SAE.

Last April 1997, the Department of Commerce arranged a return visit to the Netherlands, Belgium and Italy by 20 US companies, organizing a total of nearly 350 meetings during the trips.Plans for a high profile European Pavilion at SAE 98, with a focus on specific sub-sectors are already on hand.

Similar missions to the US by SMEs from other sectors are also under consideration.

In due course SMEs will be able to access on-line support for their own efforts to prepare for transatlantic partnership via a Transatlantic Small Business Initiative Web site.

For further contact about this initiative, please contact the US Department of Commerce or in Brussels :

Ms Anna Sodro, Directorate General XXIII/B-3
Rue de la Loi 200
B-1049 Brussels
Tel : (32) (2) 296-5893
Fax : (32) (2) 296-7558

CHAPTER 5
KEY PEOPLE DEALING WITH THE USA/NORTH AMERICA AT THE EUROPEAN COMMISSION LEVEL

The European Commission represents the Executive Branch " Government " of the Member States. There are (20) twenty Commissioners.

The President of the Commission is Mr Jacques Santer (Luxembourg).

Commissionners are designated by the respective national governments for a period of 5 years. The present Commission started on January 7, 1995.

The President of the Commission is assisted by 3 Vice-Presidents.

Commissioners are responsible for 24 Directorates General as well as other services.

The highest ranking official of the Commission for External Relations with North America is Sir Leon Brittan, Vice-President of the EU Commission. His counterpart in the USA is the United States Trade Representative (USTR).

Sir Leon Brittan, Vice-President of the European Commission
Rue de la Loi 200
B-1049 Brussels
Tel : (32) (2) 295-2514 & 295-2610
Fax : (32) (2) 296-0745 & 296-6002

Mr Ivan ROGERS, Chief of Cabinet of Sir Leon Brittan
Tel : (32) (2) 296-0125 & 295-2393
Fax : (32) (2) 396-0745 & 296-6002

Mr Simon FRASER, Deputy Chief of Cabinet of Sir Leon Brittan
Tel : (32) (2) 296-6453
Fax : (32) (2) 296-0745

Depending on the issues, the Office of Sir Leon Brittan should be able to point you in the right direction for further contact with other Commissioners and/or Directorates General.

Without going into the specificities of particular issues, one good start at the European Commission level is Directorate General I (DG I) responsible for External Relations : Commercial Policy and Relations with North America, the Far East, Australia and New Zealand, namely :

- Directorate B : "Relations with North America, Australia, New Zealand, NAFTA and APEC"
- Directorate D : "Sectoral Commercial Questions, Market Access"
- Directorate G : "WTO, OECD, Commercial Questions with respect to Agriculture and Fisheries; Export Credit Policy"

- Directorate General IA (DG IA) "External relations : European and the New Independent States, Common Foreign and Security Policy and External Missions", namely :
  - Directorate A : "Multilateral Relations"
  - Directorate F : "Human and Financial Resources and Coordination"

- Directorate General III (DG III) "Industry", namely :
  - Directorate A : "Industrial Policy"
  - Directorate C : "Industrial affairs I : Basic Industries"
  - Directorate E : "Industrial Affairs III : Concumer Goods Industries"

- Directorate General IV (DG IV) "Competition", namely :
  - Directorate A : "General Competition Policy and Coordination"
  - Directorate G : "State Aids"

- Directorate General V (DG V) "Employment, Industrial relations and Social Affairs", namely :
  - Directorate E : "Social Policy and Action"

- Directorate General VI (DG VI) "Agriculture", namely :
  - Directorate H : "International Affairs relating to Agriculture"

- Directorate General VII (DG VII) "Transport", namely :
  - Directorate A : "International Relations and Transeuropean Transport and Infrastructure Networks"
  - Directorate C : "Air transport"

- Directorate General VIII (DG VIII) "Development (External Relations and Development Cooperation with Africa, the Caribbean and the Pacific - Lomé Convention)"
- Directorate General XI (DG XI) "Environment, Nuclear Safety and Civil Protection", namely :
    - Directorate A : "General and International Matters"
    - Directorate E : "Industry and Environment"

- Directorate General XIV (DGXIV) " Fisheries ", namely :
    - Directorate B : "International Fisheries Organizations and Fisheries Agreements"
- Directorate General XV "Internal Market and Financial Services", namely :
    - Directorate A : "General Matters and Coordination, Free Movement of Persons and Direct Taxation"
- Directorate General XVII (DG XVII) "Energy", namely :
    - Directorate C : "Industries and Markets : Non-fossil Energy"
- Directorate General XXI (DG XXI) "Customs and Indirect Taxation", namely :
    - Directorate A : "General Matters"
- Directorate General XXII (DG XXII) "Education, Training and Youth", namely :
    - Directorate C : "Cooperation with Non-Member Countries, Action in the field of Youth, Publications and Information"

Directorate-General I (DG I) External Economic Relations : Commercial Policy and Relations with North America, the Far East, Australia and New Zealand

Mr Hans Friedrich Beseler - Director General
Tel : (32) (2) 295-2322 / 299-0097
DG:01

Mr Gérard Depayre - Deputy Director General
Tel : (32) (2) 295-7090 / 299-0085
DG:01
Responsibilities : Relations with North America and NAFTA

➤**Directorate B "Relations with North America, Australia, New Zealand, NAFTA and APEC"**
Mr Ove Juul Jorgensen - Director
Tel : (32) (2) 299-1531 / 295-5418
DG:01/B

➤*Unit 01 "United States of America"*
Mr Eric Hayes - Head of Unit
Tel : (32) (2) 299-1699 / 299-1701
DG:01/B/01

Mr Gunnar Wiegand - Deputy Head of unit
Tel : (32) (2) 296-3110
DG:01/B/01

Mr Hans Berend Feddersen
Tel : (32) (2) 296-3110
DG:01/B/01
Responsibilities : Macro Economic Aspects (including Monetary); Transatlantic Business Dialogue; IMF

Mr Andrew Byrne
Tel : (32) (2) 299-0027
DG:01/B/01
Responsibilities : Development, Agriculture, Fisheries, EU-US Political Dialogue on the Middle East, Mashreq, Maghreb and Africa

Mrs Milvia van Rij Brizzi
Tel : (32) (2) 299-0191
DG:01/B/01
Responsibilities : Environment, Energy; Euratom and Proliferation; Relations USA-Latin America (including Extra Territorial Legislation) and Fight Against Drugs; NAFTA and NAFTA, Enlargement, EU-US Progress Report.

Mr Michael Pulch
Tel : (32) (2) 295-5255
DG:01/B/01
Responsibilities : Summits EU-USA, Common Foreign Security Policy Correspondent , Preparation and Follow-Up on Ministerial Meetings, Relations USA-Middle East and Iran, Non proliferation, Disarmament, National Security, USA legislation, defense industry, aviation

Mr Americo Beviglia Zampetti
Tel : (32) (2) 296-5568
DG:01/B/01
Responsibilities : World Trade Organization (WTO), US Trade Legislation, Anti-Dumping, Competition

Mr Lars-Orlof Hollner
Tel : (32) (2)295-2604
DG:01/B/01
Responsibilities : Information Technology, Telecommunications, Industrial Sectors (Automobiles, Steels, SMEs); Agriculture; Anti-Dumping.

Mr Gérard Mac Polin
Tel : (32) (2) 299-0107
DG:01/B/01
Responsibilities : Financing Specific US Measures, EU-US Interdepartmental Group, Office Management, Maritime Transport, Shipbuilding

➢**Directorate D " Sectoral Commercial Questions, Market Access "**
➢*Unit 03 " New Technologies, Intellectual Property and Public Procurement"*
Mr Peter Berz
Tel : (32) (2) 296-2008
DG:01/D/03
Responsibilities : USA, General Coordination of Technical Assistance Programs, Copyright and Related Rights, Information Society

➢**Directorate G " WTO, OECD, Commercial Questions with respect to Agriculture and Fisheries; Export Credit Policy "**
➢*Unit 01 " Multilateral Commercial Policies and WTO and OECD Matters "*
Mr Bruno Julien Malvy
Tel : (32) (2) 299-2001
DG:01/G/01
Responsibilities : Institutional and Legal Matters; Settlement of Disputes; Action Plan EU/US.

Directorate General IA (DG IA) " External Political Relations : Europe, the New Independent States, Common Foreign and Security Policy and External Missions "

➢*Unit 04 " External Policy : European Correspondent "*
Mr Thomas Frellesen
Tel : (32) (2) 296-9361
DG:01A//04
Responsibilities : USA

➢**Directorate A " Multilateral Relations "**
➢*Unit 01 "Security Aspects"*
Mr Giancarlo Chevallard - Head of Unit
Tel : (32) (2) 296-5081 / 295-1797
DG:01A/A/01
Responsibilities :G7, United States

➢*Unit 03 "United Nations"*
Mr Ulrich Knüppel - Head of Unit
Tel : (32) (2) 299-57057 / 295-1884
DG:01A/A/03
Responsibilities : Horizontal Aspects; UN Work related to Security, Trade, Economic and Financial Issues; Agriculture; Food; Drugs; North America

Directorate General II (DG II) "Economic and Financial Affairs"

➤**Directorate F " Human and Financial Resources and Coordination "**
➤*Unit 02 " Budgetary Resources and Controls "*
Mr Michel Biart
Tel : (32) (2) 299-3436
DG:02/F/02
Responsibilities : USA Coordination of Economic Forecasts

Directorate General III (DG III) " Industry "

➤**Directorate A " Industrial Policy "**
➤*Unit 01 " International Relations in the Industrial and Technological Fields "*
Mr Carsten Chittek
Tel : (32) (2)296-9271
DG:03/A/01
Responsibilities : Relations with USA

➤*Unit 05 " Industrial Problems Related to Environmental Legislation "*
Mr Vlassios Venner
Tel : (32) (2) 295-5361
DG:03/A/05
Responsibilities : International Dimension : Follow-Up and Analysis of Strategic Areas in US (Aspects Related to Innovation and Information Society). G7 Follow-Up

➤**Directorate C " Industrial Affairs I : Basic Industries "**
➤*Unit 01 " Steel "*
Mr Ferdinando Marchioro
Tel : (32) (2) 295-5929 / 295-5440
DG:03/C/01
Responsibilities : North America, NAFTA, WTO, OECD, Steel Committee.

➤**Directorate E : " Industrial Affairs III : Consumer Goods Industries "**
➤*Unit 05 " Automobiles and Other Road Vehicles and Tractors "*
Mrs Sabine Weyand
Tel : (32) (2) 296-0143
DG:03/E/05
Responsibilities : USA

Directorate General IV (DG IV) " Competition "

➤**Directorate A " General Competition Policy and Coordination "**
➤*Unit 03 " International Aspects "*
Mrs Brona Carton
Tel : (32) (2) 295-9189
DG:04/A/03
Responsibilities : Relations with Countries of North America

➤**Directorate G " States Aids "**
➤*Unit 04 " Industry Aid I - Steel, Non-ferrous Metals, Mining, Shipbuilding, Automobiles and Synthetic Fibers "*
Mr Emmanuel Cremers
Tel : (32) (2) 295-2166
DG:04/G/04
Responsibilities : "Steel and Non-Ferrrous Metals", Relations with USA.

Directorate General V (DG V) " Employment, Industrial relations and Social affairs "

➤**Directorate E " Social Policy and Action "**
➤*Unit 04 " External Relations and International Organizations "*
Mr Troels Kroyer
Tel : (32) (2) 296-0633
DG:05/E/04
Responsibilities : US

Directorate General VI (DG VI) " Agriculture "

➤**Directorate H " International Affairs Relating to Agriculture"**
➤*Unit 01 "GATT, WTO and United-States of America"*
Mrs Mary Minch - Head of Unit
Tel : (32) (2) 296-1651
DG:06/H/01
Responsibilities : Application of the General Agreement

Mr Lars Berners
Tel : (32) (2) 296-1338
DG:06/H/01
Responsibilities : Membership to WTO, Tariffs Negotiations

Directorate General VII (DG VII) " Transport "

➢**Directorate A " International Relations and Transeuropean Transport and Infrastructure Networks "**
➢*Unit 01 " International Relations "*
Mr Detlev Boeing
Tel : (32) (2) 296-8366
DG:07/A/01
Responsibilities :United States, Air transport, Legal and Institutional Questions

➢**Directorate C " Air transport "**
➢*Unit 01 " Air Transport Policy "*
Mr Ludolf Van Hasselt
Tel : (32) (2) 296-8436
DG:07/C/01
Responsibilities : External Relations, USA International Organizations; Allocation of Slots, Freight

Directorate General VIII (DG VIII) " Development (External relations and Development Cooperation with Africa, the Caribbean and the Pacific - Lomé Convention) "

➢*Unit 01 "Forecasting and Programming, Macro economic Aspects and Support for Structural Adjustment "*
Mrs Christine Bakker
Tel : (32) (2) 299-2683
DG:08//01
Responsibilities : Relations and Coordination with Other Donors : General Coordination; USA

Mr Aslam Aziz
Tel : (1) (202) 862-9500
DG:08//01
Responsibilities : Relations with USAID - Seconded to Washington Delegation

Directorate General XI (DG XI) " Environment, Nuclear Safety and Civil Protection "

➢**Directorate A " General and International Matters "**
➢*Unit 04 "International Affairs, Trade and Environment"*
Mrs Danièle Smadja - Head of Unit
Tel : (32) (2) 296-9511 / 299-2236
DG:11/A/04
Responsibilities : UNCSD, UNEP, UNGA, OECD, ECE Regular and Extraordinary Ministerial Meetings, Regular Sessions, Intersessional and Preparatory Meetings. Trade and Environment - WTO, OECD, UNEP, UNCTAD, Ministerial and Regular Meetings. Bilateral Relations with the USA on Environmental Policy; Organization and Management

➢**Directorate E " Industry and Environment "**
➢*Unit 03 " Waste Management "*
Mr Emilio Canda Moreno
Tel : (32) (2) 299-0321
DG:11/E/03
Responsibilities : Packaging Directive; Environmental Technologies : Clean Technologies, Recycling Technologies; Waste Treatment; LIFE Coordination; Structural and Cohesion Funds; UNEP; USA

Directorate General XIV (DGXIV) " Fisheries "

➢**Directorate B " International Fisheries Organizations and Fisheries Agreements"**
➢*Unit 02 " Baltic, North Atlantic and North Pacific "*
Mr Friedrich Wieland
Tel : (32) (2) 296-3205
DG:14/B/02
Responsibilities : Fisheries Relations and Agreements with the USA

Directorate General XV " Internal Market and Financial Services"

➤Directorate A " General Matters and Coordination, Free movement of Persons and Direct Taxation "
➤*Unit 02 " External Dimension of the Internal Market and Financial Services"*
Mr Jens Viberg
Tel : (32) (2) 296-3034
DG:15/A/02
Responsibilities : Coordination of Bilateral Relations with Non-Member Countries US; Market Access Strategy; Electronic Commerce; General Issues Relevant to the DG XV, incl. WTO

Directorate General XVII (DG XVII) " Energy "

➤Directorate C " Industries and Markets : Non-Fossil Energy "
➤*Unit 04 " Nuclear Conventions "*
Mr Ralph Lennartz
Tel : (32) (2) 296-3620
DG:17/C/04
Responsibilities : Preparation of Negotiations and Management of Nuclear Agreements with : USA

Directorate General XXI (DG XXI) "Customs and Indirect Taxation"

➤Directorate A " General Matters "
➤*Unit 03 " International Matters "*
Mrs Genoveva Ruiz Calavera
Tel : (32) (2)+ 2950793
DG:21/A/03
Responsibilities : General Questions

Directorate General XXII (DG XXII) "Education, Training and Youth"

➢**Directorate C "Cooperation with non-member Countries, action in the field of Youth, Publications and Information"**

➢*Unit 01 "Cooperation with Non-Member Countries on Education and Vocational Training, including Tempus and the European Training Foundation"*

Mrs Constance Meldrum
Tel : (32) (2) 296-2534
DG:22/C/01

CHAPTER 6
KEY PEOPLE DEALING WITH THE USA
AT THE EUROPEAN PARLIAMENT LEVEL

The European Parliament is comprised of 626 members elected by suffrage for a period of 5 years. The next elections will take place in 1999.

The European Parliament exerts an increasing influence in the legislative process of the EU. It adopts the budget, supervises the activities of the Commission and the Council, adapts or cancels international agreements, and in some areas enjoys a legislative co-decision power.

Here is a breakdown of the European Parliament Members by countries :

Ranking by order of importance	# of EPMS	% of total
Germany	99	15.8
France	87	13.9
Italy	87	13.9
United Kingdom	87	13.9
Spain	64	10.2
Netherlands	31	5.0
Belgium	25	4.0
Greece	25	4.0
Portugal	25	4.0
Sweden	22	3.5
Austria	21	3.4
Finland	16	2.6
Denmark	16	2.6
Ireland	15	2.4
Luxembourg	6	0.1
	626	99.3

A. Political Groups

European Parliament Members are not regrouped by national delegations, but according to the Political Groups they belong to :

Political Groups are important in the works of the Parliament, both from a political and organizational viewpoint.

There are 8 Political Groups represented within the European Parliament :

- 1. Group of the Party of European Socialists (PSE) : 217 members or 34.7 % of total.
- 2. Group of the European People's Party (Christian Democratic Group) (PPE) : 173 members or 27.6 % of total.
- 3. Group Union for Europe (UFE) : 55 members or 8.8 % of total.
- 4. Group of the European Liberal Democrat and Reform Party (ELDR) : 52 members or 8.3 % of total.
- 5. Confederal Group of the European United Left/Nordic Green Left (GUE/NGL) 33 members or 5.2 % of total.
- 6. The Green Group in the European Parliament (V) : 27 members or 4.3 % of total.
- 7. Group of the European Radical Alliance (ARE) : 20 members or 3.2 % of total.
- 8. Group of Independents for Europe of Nations (I-EDN) : 18 members or
  2.9 % of total.

There are also 31 Non-Attached (NI) members.

The different Political Groups have their own Secretariat based in Brussels and the amount of funding which each Secretariat receives depends on the number of members belonging to each group.

B. Committees

Work of the Parliament is prepared by 20 specialized Committees, and 3 Sub-Committees. In addition to these Permanent Committees, the EP can also appoint Temporary Committees or Investigative Committees to examine certain specific problems.

Parliamentary Committees elaborate replies to the legislative proposals coming from the European Commission, and they can also initiate reports although the latter are not part of the legislative process. Committees are totally free to organize public hearings, at which time experts are called in to give their advice on the technical aspects of particular issues.

Members of the European Parliament can be contacted either in Brussels or Strasbourg

Brussels :
Rue Belliard 97-113
B-1047 Brussels
Tel : (32) (2) 284-2111
Fax : (32) (2) 230-6933

Strasbourg :
Palais de l' Europe
Avenue de l' Europe
F-67006 Strasbourg Cedex
Tel : (33) (3) 88 17 40 01
Fax : (33) (3) 88 17 48 60

For the sake of this Guide, we only show hereafter the breakdown of the Committee for External Economic Relations (Referred to as C6), as it is the one most likely to be involved in any US-EU matters.

Depending on the issues, assuredly Committees should be contacted. For details about other Committees, the reader is referred to the European Parliament Secretariat in Luxembourg :

Centre Européen
Plateau du Kirchberg BP 1601
L-2929 Luxembourg
Tel : (352) 43001
Fax : (352) 434072

We also show (further on) the breakdown of the Delegation for Relations with the United States (D11). Interparliamentary Delegations are established by the European Parliament and maintain relations with one country or group of countries that are not members of the EU.

C6 Commission for External Economic Relations

President :
Luciana Castellina (Italy/GUE/NGL)

Vice-Presidents :
Fernando Moniz (Portugal/PSE)
André Sainjon (France/ARE)
Peter Kittelmann (Germany/PPE)

Members :
Yvan M. Blot (France/NI)
Pier Ferdinando Casini (Italy/PPE)
Dietrich Elchlepp (Germany/PSE)
Alexander C. Falconer (UK/PSE)
Conceptio Ferrer (Spain/PPE)
Karl Habsburg-Lothringen (Austria/PPE)
Michael J. Hindley (UK/PSE)
Roger Karoutchi (France/UPE)
Wolfgang Kreiss-Dörfler (Germany/V)
Erika Mann (Germany/PSE)
Graham Mather (UK/PPE)
Ana Miranda de Lage (Spain/PSE)
Riccardo Papakyriazis (Greece/PSE)
Elly Plooij-van Gorsel (Netherlands/ELDR)
Manuel Porto (Portugal/PPE)
Konrad K. Schwaiger (Germany/PPE)
Alex Smith (UK/PSE)
Dominique F.C. Souchet (France/EDN)
Antonio Tajani (Italy/UPE)
Jaime Valdivielso de Cué (Spain/PPE)

Breakdown by Countries :

Austria	1
France	4
Germany	5
Greece	1
Italy	4
Netherlands	1
Portugal	2
Spain	3
UK	4
	—
	25

Luciana Castellina   Italy
Camera de Deputati
Via Offici del Vicario 9-A
I-00186 Roma
Tel : (39) (6) 67604200 / 67604949
Tel Bru : (32) (2) 284-5151
Fax : (39) (6) 67604925
Fax Bru : (32) (2) 284-9151
Fax Str : (33) (3) 88179151
E-mail : mc4746@mclink.it

Fernando Moniz   Portugal
Augusto Correia n° 54
P-4760 V.N. de Famalicas
Tel : (351) (52) 72346
Fax : (351) (52) 73458
Fax Bru : (32) (2) 284-9683
Fax Str : (33) (3) 88179683

André Sainjon   France
Rue des Vendanges 22
F-83270 Saint Cyr sur Mer
Tel : (33) (4) 94321619
Fax : (33) (1) 48576313
Fax Bru : (32) (2) 284-9497
Fax Str : (33) (3) 88179497

Peter Kittelman   Germany
Im Dol 15
D-14195 Berlin
Tel : (49) (30) 8326764
Tel Bru : (32) (2) 284-5312
Fax : (49) (30) 8318028
Fax Bru : (32) (2) 284-9312
Fax Str : (33) (3) 88179312

Yvan M. Blot   France
Avenue de la Paix 35
F-67070 Strasbourg Cedex
Tel : (33) (3) 88156867 Post 18 20
Fax : (33) (3) 88379427
Fax Bru : (32) (2) 284-9266
Fax Str : (33) (3) 88179266

Pier Fernando Casini   Italy
Stradda Maggiore 71
I-40125 Bologna
Tel : (39) (51) 342664
Fax : (39) (51) 343936
Fax Bru : (32) (2) 284-9852
Fax Str : (33) (3) 88179852

Diedrich Elchlepp   Germany
Schwarzwaldstrasse 26
D-79211 Denzlingen
Tel : (49) (7666) 3495
Fax : (49) (7666) 288046
Fax Bru : (32) (2) 284-9506
Fax Str : (33) (3) 88179506

Alexandre C. Falconer   United Kingdom
Park Road 4
GB-KY11 2PA Rosyth Fife
Te : (44) (1383) 419330
Fax : (44) (1383) 417957
Fax Bru : (32) (2) 284-9509
Fax Str : (33) (3) 88179509

Conception Ferrer   Spain
Sardenya 492 altell
E-08025 Barcelona
Tel : (34) (3) 4568970
Tel Bru : (32) (2) 284-5982
Fax : (34) (3) 4350330
Fax Bru : (32) (2) 284-9982
Fax Str : (33) (3) 88179982

Karl Habsburg-Lothringen   Austria
Auerspergstrasse 36
A-5020 Salzburg
Tel : (43) (662) 882730
Fax : (43) (662) 87001616
Fax Bru : (32) (2) 284-9772
Fax Str : (33) (3) 88179772

Michael J. Hindley   United Kingdom
Commercial Road 27
GB-BB6 7HX Great Harwood
Tel : (44) (1254) 887017
Fax : (44) (1254) 393379
Fax Bru : (32) (2) 284-9507
Fax Str : (33) (3) 88179507
E-mail : michael.hindley@mcr1.poptel.ord.uk

Roger Karoutchi   France
Rue Nungesser et Coli 4
F-92100 Boulogne
Tel : (33) (1) 49556305
Fax : (33) (1) 49556484
Fax Bru : (32) (2) 284-5161
Fax Str : (33) (3) 88175161

Wolfgang Kreiss-Dörfler   Germany
Alfred Schmidt Strasse 18
D-81379 München
Tel : (49) (89) 7243840
Fax : (49) (89) 774077
Fax Bru : (32) (2) 284-9110
Fax Str : (33) (3) 88179110

Erika Mann   Germany
Klostergut Schachtenbeck
D-37581 Bad Gandersheim
Tel : (49) (5382) 2667
Tel Bru : (32) (2) 284-5191
Fax : (49) (5382) 2641
Fax Bru : (32) (2) 284-9191
Fax Str : (33) (3) 88179191

Graham Mather   United Kingdom
European Policy Forum
Queen Anne's Gate 20
GB-SW1H 9AA London
Tel : (44) (171) 2220733
Fax : (44) (171) 2220554
Fax Bru : (32) (2) 284-9291
Fax Str : (33) (3) 88179291
E-mail : 100541.1060@compuserve.com

Ana Miranda de Lage   Spain
Plaza de las Cortes 9
E-28014 Madrid
Tel : (34) (1) 4247556
Tel Bru : (32) (2) 284-5883
Fax Bru : (32) (2) 284-9883
Fax Str : (33) (3) 88179883

Riccardo Nencini   Italy
Via Castellare 6
I-50031 Barberino Mugello
Tel : (39) (55) 8417834
Fax Bru : (32) (2) 284-9713
Fax Str : (33) (3) 88179713

Nikolaos Papakyriazis   Greece
Anaximandrou 100
GR-542 50 Thessaloniki
Tel : (30) (31) 303078
Fax : (30) (31) 264467
Fax Bru : (32) (2) 284-9570
Fax Str : (33) (3) 88179570

Elly Plooij van Gorsel   Netherlands
Hoge Nieuwstraat 24
NL-2514 EL Den Haag
Tel : (31) (70) 3647447
Fax : (31) (70) 3451026
Fax Bru : (32) (2) 284-9608
Fax Str : (33) (3) 88179608
E-mail : 106017.3650@compuserve.com

Manuel Porto   Portugal
Faculdade Direito de Coimbra
Patio de Universidade
P-3049 Coimbra Codex
Tel : (351) (39) 22113
Tel Bru : (32) (2) 284-5372
Fax : (351) (39) 23353
Fax Bru : (32) (2) 284-9372
Fax Str : (33) (3) 88179372

Konrad K. Schwaiger   Germany
Stadtgrabenstrasse 17
D-76646 Bruchsal
Tel : (49) (7251) 12175
Tel Bru : (32) (2) 284-5384
Fax : (49) (7251) 86275
Fax Bru : (32) (2) 284-9384
Fax Str : (33) (3) 88179384

Alex Smith   United Kingdom
Kersland Foot 35
Girdle Toll
GB-KA11 1BP Irvine (Scotland)
Tel : (44) (1294) 216704
Fax : (44) (1294) 280141
Fax Bru (32) (2) 284-9208
Fax Str : (33) (3) 88179208
E-mail : asmithmep@enterprise.net

Dominique F.C. Souchet   France
La Popelinière
F-85400 Sainte-Gemme
Fax Bru : (32) (2) 284-9246
Fax Str : (33) (3) 88179246

Antonio Tajani   Italy
Via T. Salvani 51
I-00197 Roma
Tel : (39) (6) 6798648
Fax Bru : (32) (2) 284-9396
Fax Str : (33) (3) 88179396

Jaime Valdivielso de Cué   Spain
Altzarrate 10
E-01400 Llodio
Tel : (34) (4) 6726650
Fax : (34) (4) 6722999
Fax Bru : (32) (2) 284-9644
Fax Str : (33) (3) 88179644

KEY PEOPLE DEALING WITH THE USA
AT THE EUROPEAN PARLIAMENT

D11 : Delegation for Relations with the United States

President :
Alan John Donnelly (UK/PSE)

Vice Presidents :
Bryan M.D. Cassidy (UK/PPE)
Lucio Manisco (Italy/GUE/NGL)

Members :
Nuala Ahern (Ireland/V)
Javier Areitio Toledo (Spain/PPE)
Mary Banotti (Ireland/PPE)
Elmar Brok (Germany/PPE)
Jean-Pierre Cot (France/PSE)
Jacques Donnay (France/UPE)
Willi Görlach (Germany/PSE)
Ilona Graenitz (Austria/PSE)
Mark Killilea (Ireland/UPE)
Karla M.H. Peijs (Netherlands/PPE)
Elly Plooij van Gorsel (Netherlands/ELDR)
Barry H. Seal (UK/PSE)
Josep Verdi I Aldea (Spain/PSE)

Breakdown by Countries :

Austria	1
France	2
Germany	2
Ireland	3
Italy	1
Netherlands	2
Spain	2
United Kingdom	3
	—
	16

Alan John Donnelly   United Kingdom
South View 1
GB-Jarrow
Tel : (44) (191) 4897643
Fax Bru : (32) (2) 284-9202
Fax Str : (33) (3) 88179202
E-mail : alan.donnelly@ping.be

Brian M.D. Cassidy   United Kingdom
Esmont Court 11
Thackeray Street
GB-W8 5HB London
Tel : (44) (171) 9373558
Tel Bru : (32) (2) 284-5236
Fax : (44) (171) 9373558
Fax Bru : (32) (2) 284-9236
Fax Str : (33) (3) 88179236

Lucio Manisco   Italy
Via C. Beccaria 88
I-00196 Roma
Tel : (39) (6) 3613342
Fax : (39) (6) 3613342
Fax Bru : (32) (2) 284-9180
Fax Str : (33) (3) 88179180

Nuala Ahern   Ireland
La Touche Place
IRL- Greystone Co.
Wicklow
Tel : (353) (1) 2876574
Tel Bru : (32) (2) 284-5139/284-7134
Fax : (353) (1) 2872638
Fax Bru : (32) (2) 284-9139
Fax Str : (33) (3) 88179139
E-mail : 106114.173@compuserve.com

Javier Areitio Toledo   Spain
La Moraleja
Calle Camino Viejo 77
E-28109 Alcobendas, Madrid
Tel : (34) (1) 6502986
Fax : (34) (1) 6506089
Fax Bru : (32) (2) 284-9754
Fax Str : (33) (3) 88179754

Mary Banotti   Ireland
Cambridge Avenue 8
Ringsend
IRL- Dublin 4
Tel : (353) (1) 6680341
Fax : (353) (1) 6796593
Fax Bru : (32) (2) 284-9225
Fax Str : (33) (3) 88179225
E-mail : mbanotti@arcadis.be

Elmar Brok   Germany
Fr. Verleger Strasse 3
D-33602 Bielefeld
Tel : (49) (521) 64749
Tel Bru : (32) (2) 284-5323
Fax : (49) (521) 177427
Fax Bru : (32) (2) 284-9323
Fax Str : (33) (3) 88179323

Jean-Pierre Cot   France
Coise St-Jean-Pied-Gauthier
F-73800 Montmélian
Tel : (33) (4) 79288016
Tel Bru : (32) (2) 284-5787
Fax : (33) (4) 79288016
Fax Bru (32) (2) 284-9787
Fax Str (33) (3) 88179787
E-mail : jean.pierre.cot@infoboard.be

Jacques Donnay   France
Avenue du Maréchal Leclerc 12
F-59110 La Madeleine
Tel : (33) (3) 20551875
Fax : (33) (3) 20635228
Fax Bru : (32) (2) 284-9168
Fax Str : (33) (3) 88179168

Willi Görlach   Germany
Oberpforte 2
D-35510 Butzbach
Tel : (49) (6033) 60292
Fax : (49) (6033) 60292
Fax Bru : (32) (2) 284-9174
Fax Str : (33) (3) 88179174
E-mail : 101500.1512@compuserve.com

Ilona Graenitz   Austria
Lustenauerstrasse 9
A-4020 Linz
Tel : (43) (732) 782914
Fax Bru : (32) (2) 284-9718
Fax Str : (33) (3) 88179718

Mark Killilea   Ireland
Caherhugh House
Belclare
IRL- Tuam Co. Galway
Tel : (353) (93) 55414
Fax : (353) (93) 55386
Fax Bru : (32) (2) 284-9520
Fax Str : (33) (3) 88179520

Karla M.H. Peijs   Netherlands
Achtersloot 53
NL-3401 NS Ijsselstein
Tel : (31) (30) 6888556
Fax : (31) (30) 6870140
Fax Bru : (32) (2) 284-9861
Fax Str : (33) (3) 88179861
E-mail : 101376.2016@compuserve.com

Elly Plooij-van Gorsel   Netherlands
Hoge Nieuwstraat 24
NL-2514 EL Den Haag
Tel : (31) (70) 3647447
Fax : (31) (70) 3641026
Fax Bru : (32) (2) 284-9608
Fax Str : (33) (3) 88179608
E-mail : 106017.3650@compuserve.com

Barry H. Seal   United Kingdom
Brookfields Farm
Brookfields Road - Wyke
GB-BD12 9LU Bedford
Tel : (44) (1274) 752091
Fax : (44) (1274) 752092
Fax Bru : (32) (2) 284-9401
Fax Str : (33) (3) 88179401

Josep Verde I Aldea   Spain
Enric Granados 95 3° 1a
E-08008 Barcelona
Tel : (34) (3) 2182270
Fax : (34) (3) 4159919
Fax Bru : (32) (2) 284-9914
Fax Str : (33) (3) 88179914
E-mail : j.verde@readisoft.es

CHAPTER 7
US ASSOCIATIONS REPRESENTED
IN BRUSSELS

American Electronics Association
601 Pennsylvania Avenue NW
North Building, Suite 600
Washington DC. 20004
Tel : (1) (202) 682-9110
Fax : (1) (202) 682-9111

American Electronics Association Europe - AEA Europe
Rue des Drapiers 40
B - 1050 Brussels
Tel : (32) (2) 502-7015
Fax : (32) (2) 502-6734
e-mail: stephany holmgren@aeanet.org.
Web site: http:\\www.aeanet.org.
Ms Stephany Holmgren, Director

The American Electronics Association (AEA) is a not-for-profit organization that directly represents 3,000 electronics manufacturers in all segments of the global electronics industry, from software and semiconductors to computers, instrumentation and communications systems via 20 AEA offices around the world.

AEA Europe is committed to fostering a favorable business environment for the continued success and growth of its members' operations in Europe. Through its network of information and services, AEA Europe represents its members' concerns with AEA-US and acts as an advocate with European and US government agencies on issues impacting European business.

In 1991, the AEA established its Brussels office in order to help high-tech companies take full advantage of the opportunities arising from the expanding European market. AEA Europe's objective is to provide its members with the following benefits:

- Access to the latest information on issues affecting the business environment.

- Opportunity to develop industry policy positions and communicate them to the relevant government institutions.
- Networking events in order to facilitate information flow and develop industry contacts.

AEA Europe offers the following network of information and services to its member companies:

- Free attendance of the 36 meetings/year of 6 policy working groups.
- Standards: Certification
- Internet: Electronic Commerce
- International Technology Agreement
- Environment, Health and Safety
- Intellectual Property
- Customs.
- Free or reduced cost attendance at special events on topical issues.
- Free bi-monthly updates on European issues (AEA Europe Highlights).
- Reduced cost to AEA Europe publications (Environmental Bulletin, IPR Guide, ...)
- Free or reduced participation in networking events (Annual Conference).
- Free copies of issue-specific documents from archives.
- Free assistance with light consulting, business facilitation and inter-member or service provider referrals.

■ APA. The Engineered Wood Association
Grote Steenweg, 264
B-2600 Berchem
Tel : (32) (3) 440-6838
Fax : (32) (3) 440 0840
Mr M. G. Robert Verhorst, Overseas Director

■ Personal Computer Memory Card International Association - PCMIA
Avenue Marcel Thiry, 204
B-1200 Brussels
Tel: (32) (2) 774-9620
Fax: (32) (2) 774-9690
E-mail: 100113.1555 @compuserve.com
http:/www.pc card.com
Mr Bill Lempevis, CEO & Chief Operating Officer.
Mr Anthony Wutka, President of the Board of Directors

Association for Computer Machinery (ACM) - European Service Center
108 Cowley Road
UK - Oxford OX4 IJS
Tel : (44) (1865) 382-338
Fax : (44) (1865) 381-338

■ Association of Management Consulting Firms - (AMCF)
Avenue Marcel Thiry, 204
B-1200 Brussels
Tel : (32) (2) 774-9528
Fax : (32) (2) 774-9690
Mr Dudley Smith, President
Mr Alfons Westgeest, Director

■ American Re-Insurance Company
American-Re - Plaza 1
555 College Road East
P.O. Box 5241
Princeton, N.J. 08543
Tel : (1) (609) 243-4200
Fax : (1) (609) 243-4257

Committee of American Insurers in Europe (CAIE)
Avenue des Pléiades, 19
B-1200 Brussels
Tel : (32) (2) 772-5858
Fax : (32) (2) 772-5308
Mr Claude Dierkens, Secretary

■ **Society of Plastics Engineers European Office - SPE**
Avenue Marcel Thiry, 204
B-1200 Brussels
Tel : (32) (2) 774-9630
Fax : (32) (2) 774-9690
E-mail: spe@ eyam.be
Ms Fanna Melker, Director Europe

■ **Motion Picture Association of America, Inc.**
1600 Eye Street, NW
Washington DC. 20006
Tel: (1) (202) 293-1966

15503 Ventura Boulevard
Encino, CA 91436
Tel: (1) (818) 995-6600
Mr Jack Valenti, President/CEO/MPAA/MPA

Motion Picture Association
Avenue de Tervuren 270-272
B-1150 Brussels
Tel : (32) (2) 778-2711
Fax : (32) (2) 778-2700
Mr Christopher Marcich, Senior Vice President
Mr Michael Bartholomew, Director Community Affairs

The Motion Picture Association of America (MPAA) and its international counterpart, the Motion Picture Association, (MPA) serve as the voice and advocate of the American motion picture, home video and television industries, domestically through the MPAA and internationally through the MPA.

Among its major activities, the MPA/Brussels Office, with the support of the US Headquarters in Los Angeles, California:

- Works to eliminate restrictive trade regulations and non-tariff barriers to allow free competition in the European marketplace.

- Assists in the drafting of international treaties that affect the marketing, sales, leasing, taxation and distribution of the products of the US film industry, primarily on the European continent.

- Acts as liaison between MPA's member companies and the European Commission on matters related to international commerce. The MPA

Brussels Office addresses both EU and national legislation and regulatory proposals which would impact the production and distribution of motion pictures, television programs and home video in Europe. In this capacity, it serves as a spokesman for the member companies before the Commission of the European Union and relevant EU regulatory agencies and commissions, as well as legislative bodies, executive and regulatory arms of EU and national governments. The MPA Brussels Office provides its member companies with a regular update on legislation and proposed regulatory changes that may affect the business practices of industry in Europe.

- Negotiates industry-wide agreements in Europe on matters related to the theatrical presentation, home video distribution, television syndication and transmission and retransmission of television programs and films.

- Protects the right of copyright owners, primarily on the European marketplace.

- Works with the film industries in Europe on matters of common interest designed to preserve the freedom of the marketplace.

- Directs an anti-piracy effort to protect US films and home videos from being stolen by pirates throughout Europe.

Member companies of the MPA in the USA include Buena Vista International Inc., Columbia Tristar Film Distributors International Inc., Metro-Goldwyn-Mayer Inc., Paramount Pictures Corporation, Turner Pictures, Twentieth Century Fox International Corporation, Universal International Films, Inc., and Warner Bros..

■ Motor & Equipment Manufacturers Association
P.O. Box 13966, 10 Laboratory Drive
Research Triangle Park, NC 27709-3966 USA
Tel : (1) (919) 549-4800, (1) (800) 549-MEMA
Fax : (1) (919) 549-4824

Washington Office:
1325 Pennsylvania Avenue NW, Sixth Floor
Washington DC 20004 USA
Tel : (1) (202) 393-MEMA
Fax : (1) (202) 737-3742

North American Automotive Parts Industry European Office
Avenue Marcel Thiry, 204
B-1200 Brussels
Tel : (32) (2) 774-9606
Fax : (32) (2) 774-9690
E-mail: 100113.155@compuserve.com
Mr Robert Miller, President
Mr Charles Blum, President

The Motor & Equipment Manufacturers Association (MEMA) and the Specialty Equipment Market Association (SEMA), combining a total of 3,000 member companies, opened a joint office in Brussels, Belgium, in 1992 to help their members expand business in Europe and improve communications with the European Community on trade and regulatory matters affecting US automotive manufacturers' sales in the region.

This office provides broad-based European business facilitation, market, legislative and regulatory research, and industry-government liaison services to both associations and their members.

The MEMA/SEMA office closely monitors and reports on European Union initiatives in the areas of industrial design, motor vehicle safety, and environmental protection measures and works with individual association members in expanding their original equipment and aftermarket contacts and business throughout Europe.

The office provides a monthly newsletter, European Automotive Insight.

Overview of Services

Introductory Business Service (Determining if there is a market for a given product and how that market is structured).

Initial Contact Building (Providing list of contacts, arranging meetings in Europe, making contacts on behalf of member companies, attending meetings and follow-up reporting, as appropriate).

European Marketing Advice (This includes "Europeanizing" existing promotional materials, finding target groups, advising on appropriate channels in order to reach this target such as suggesting trade shows to attend or publications in which to advertise.

Regulatory information to assist US member companies in meeting European product requirements.

Information Resource

Targeted Aftermarket Database, identifying importers, distributors, wholesalers and manufacturers' representatives for a wide range of aftermarket parts, accessories and chemical products. - Publications database, identifying suitable publications in a variety of European countries, covering all aspects of the automotive trade and consumer readership. - International Show Listings, identifying shows during the year throughout Europe.

■ Pharmaceutical Research and Manufacturers of America (PRMA)
1100 Fifteenth Street NW
Washington DC 20005

Pharmaceutical Research and Manufacturers of America (PRMA)
Hoge Wei 10
B-1930 Zaventem
Tel : (32) (2) 725-3567
Fax : (32) (2) 725-3677
E-mail: schpens@ pfizer.com
Mr Hugo Schepens, Representative in Europe

The mission of the Pharmaceutical Research and Manufacturers of America is to help the research-based pharmaceutical industry successfully meet its goal of discovering, developing and bringing to market medicines to improve human health, patient satisfaction and the quality of life around the world, as well as to reduce the overall cost of health care.

To achieve its goal, the industry aspires to foster a favorable environment that encourages:

- Innovative drug research.
- Swift development and approval of safe and effective drugs.
- Consumer and patient access to medicines in an open and competitive marketplace.
- Support and understanding from the public and other key constituents regarding the critical role and value of the pharmaceutical industry in

improving human health and quality of life and in reducing overall health care costs.

- Public policies that allow sufficient returns to foster continued innovation.

As the primary public advocate for the industry, PRMA helps in shaping such an external environment in close coordination with member companies by:

- Building a factual database on the value provided by the industry.
- Coordinating and leading a concerted effort to educate the public about the drug discovery and development process and the role medicines play in improving quality of life while reducing overall health care costs.
- Leading the advocacy efforts for the industry on regulatory, legislative and international issues, in close coordination with member companies.
- Working with member companies to reach agreement on and support for industry positions on important issues.
- Promoting a fair and competitive external marketplace.
- Providing selected information and other high-priority support services to member companies.
- Enhancing intellectual property protection worldwide, i.e.:
- Strengthening patent and trademark protection in industrialized nations, especially by ensuring that the exclusivity period fully compensates for regulatory delays.
- Ensuring the effective operations of the new European Medicines Evaluation Agency (EMEA)
- Eliminating counterfeiting and patent piracy
- Expediting the introduction of strong and effective patent trademark and trade secret protection in developing countries.

CHAPTER 8
US REGIONAL, STATE AND
PORT AUTHORITY OFFICES IN BRUSSELS
AND ELSEWHERE IN EUROPE

As of the date of this publication, there are a total of 30 states represented in Europe, as well as various US port cities. Because these offices are dedicated to promoting trade, investment and shipping for their state and port areas, they are in a position to offer valuable services both to American firms seeking contacts in different European countries and to European businessmen wishing information or assistance in doing business in particular parts of the United States.

For some strategic, political, economic or simply linguistic reasons, states for the most part have chosen to operate out of either Brussels, Frankfurt or London. All states represented in Europe are regrouped under the Council of American States in Europe (CASE).

US STATES REPRESENTED IN BELGIUM

In all, 10 states are represented in Belgium.

One (1) state, the state of Oklahoma, has chosen Antwerp, Belgium, as its European office.

State of Oklahoma (OK) European Office
Lambermontstraat 7
B-2000 Antwerpen
Tel : (32) (3) 240-1771
Fax : (32) (3) 240-1770
Mr Frank Roovers, Director
Mr Eric Roovers, Trade Representative

Ten (10) states have chosen Brussels, Belgium, as their European office. They are:

Arkansas
Georgia
Illinois
Kansas
Kentucky
Michigan
Minnesota
Ohio
Utah
Virginia

State of Arkansas (AR) European Office
Rue St. Georges,22-24, Bte 1
B-1050 Brussels
Tel : (32) (2) 649-6024
Fax : (32) (2) 649-4807
E-mail : 101470.1672@compuserve.com
Ms Sybille Magee, Managing Director

State of Georgia (GA) European Office
Avenue Louise,380, Bte 2
B-1050 Brussels
Tel : (32) (2) 647-7825
Fax : (32) (2) 640-6813
E-mail: invest@georgia.be
Mr James Blair, Managing Director
Mr Ryan Thornton, Deputy Director
Ms Lisa Boxy, Trade Representative

State of Illinois (IL) European Office
Blvd de la Cambre,28-30, Bte 2
B-1000 Brussels
Tel : (32) (2) 646-5730
Fax : (32) (2) 646-5511
E-mail: ileurope@compuserve.com
Mr Bart A. Smit, Managing Director
Ms Sharon L. Stead, Director Ind. Dev.

State of Kansas (KS) European Office
Avenue des Arts, 41, Bte 1
B-1040 Brussels
Tel : (32) (2) 505-0998
Fax : (32) (2) 502-2860
Mr Randy Miller, Director
Ms Katty De Coster, Trade Representative

Commonwealth of Kentucky (KY) European Office
Avenue Louise, 149, Bte 49
B-1050 Brussels
Tel : (32) (2) 535-7642
Fax : (32) (2) 535-7575
E-mail: kentucky.europe@infoboard.be
Mr Stephen C. Schulte, Director Europe

State of Michigan (MI) European Office
Avenue Louise,207, Bte 10
B-1050 Brussels
Tel : (32) (2) 645-1843
Fax : (32) (2) 645-0912
E-mail: michigan@micstate.be
Mr Dean Johnson, Managing Director
Ms Tiffany Fliss, Trade Representative

State of Minnesota (MN) European Office
Oppenheimer Wolff & Donnelly c/o Minnesota Office
Avenue Louise, 250, Bte 31
B-1050 Brussels
Tel : (32) (2) 626-0500
Fax : (32) (2) 626-0510
Mr Eric Osterweil, Trade Representative

State of Ohio (OH) European Office
Rue de la Pépinière, 1
B-1000 Brussels
Tel : (32) (2) 512-8687
Fax : (32) (2) 512-6614
E-mail: ohio.europe@infoboard.be
Mr Paul Zito, Managing Director
Ms Kerry Lydon, Assistant Director
Ms Anita Wuellner, Representative

State of Utah (UT) European Office
Benelux Office
Avenue Baron de Castro
B-1040 Brussels
Tel : (32) (2) 732-1240
Fax : (32) (2) 734-3179
Mr Frederic De Pryck, Benelux Representative

Commonwealth of Virginia (VA) European Office
Department of Agriculture and Consumer Services
Avenue Louise 479, Bte 55
Tel : (32) (2) 648-6344
Fax : (32) (2) 646-3554
Mr F.J. Schmidt, Director for Europe, Middle East and Africa

US STATE REPRESENTED IN FRANCE

State of Washington (WA)
Rue de Miromesnil, 104
F-75008 Paris
Tel : (33) (1) 44-95-72-05
Fax : (33) (1) 44-95-72-06
E-mail: 74735.435@compuserve.com
Mrs Dominique Gervais, Director

US STATES REPRESENTED IN GERMANY

Fifteen(15) states are represented in Germany.

One (1) state, the State of Massachusetts, is based in Berlin, Germany:

State of Massachusetts (MA) Berlin Office
Hallerstr. 6
D-10587 Berlin
Tel : (49) (30) 39-90-25-47
Fax : (49) (30) 39-90-25-48
E-mail: masstrade@contrib.com
Mr Bruce Greenwood, Director
Ms Claudia Seeber, Trade Specialist

One (1) state, the State of Michigan, is based in Cologne:

State of Michigan (MI) Cologne Office
Em Dau 6
D-50678 Köln
Tel : (49) (221) 93-22-255
Fax : (49) (221) 93-22-254
Mr York Weidemann, Business Development Representative

Two (2) states, the State of North Carolina and the State of Missouri, are based in Düsseldorf:

State of North Carolina (NC) European Office
Wasserstrasse 2
D-40213 Düsseldorf
Tel : (49) (211) 32-05-33
Fax : (49) (211) 13-29-54
Mr Forrest E. Rogers, European Director
Mr Tim Branscombe, Trade Director
Ms Gerda Goyer, Trade Assistant
Mrs Brigitta Kanand, Administrative Assistant

State of Missouri (MO) European Office
Herderstrasse 68
D-40237 Düsseldorf
Tel : (49) (211) 69-14-595
Fax : (49) (211) 69-14-422
Ms Sally Gladden, Director
Mr Klaus Jonas, Trade Specialist

Eight (8) states are based in Frankfurt, Germany, including:

California
Florida
Iowa
New York
Pennsylvania
South Carolina
Virginia
Wisconsin

State of California (CA) Frankfurt Office
Bockenheimer Landstrasse 97
D-60325 Frankfurt/Main
Tel : (49) (69) 743-2461
Fax : (49) (69) 745-005
Ms Trudi Schifter, Managing Director
Mr Seth page, Investment Specialist
Mr Will Leonardos Trade Manager

State of Florida (FL) European Office
Department of Commerce
Schillerstrasse 10
D-60313 Frankfurt/Main 1
Tel : (49) (69) 131-01-04
Fax : (49) (69) 131-06-47
Mr Peter C. Armstrong, Managing Director
Mr Devin V. Miller, International Marketing Manager
Ms Kathleen Harlander, Trade and Investments Coordinator

State of Iowa (IA) European Office
Development Commission
Meisengasse 8
D-60313 Frankfurt/Main 1
Tel : (49) (69) 28-38-58
Fax : (49) (69) 28-14-93
E-mail: iowa europe@compuserve.com
Mr Paul Wagner, Director & Chairman of the Council of American States in Europe (CASE)

State of New York (NY) Frankfurt Office
Bockenheimer Landstr. 39,5.OG
D-60325 Frankfurt/Main
Tel : (49) (69) 97-07-1090
Fax : (49) (69) 97-07-1091
E-mail: nys@access.de
Ms Gabriele Brennan, Director

State of Pennsylvania (PA) Frankfurt Office
Steinrutsch 7a
D-65931 Frankfurt/Main
Tel : (49) (69) 36-36-58
Fax : (49) (69) 36-37-10
E-mail: pennsylvania.info@online.de
Mr Thomas Beyer, Managing Director
Ms Ute Vogler, Assistant Director

State of South Carolina (SC) European Office
International Business Development
Wilhelm-Leuschner Strasse 9-11
D-60329 Frankfurt/Main
Tel : (49) (69) 24-29-990
Fax : (49) (69) 23-40-73
E-mail: southcarolinaeurope@online.de
Mr William McNair, Director European Office
Mr John D. Brennan, European Trade Director

State of Virginia (VA) European Office
Untermainanlage 5
D-60329 Frankfurt/Main
Tel : (49) (69) 27-39-90-0
Fax : (49) (69) 27-39-90-20
E-mail: state of virginia@compuserve.com
Mr Hans U. Schetelig, Director Europe
Mr Christian Hager, International Marketing Manager

State of Wisconsin (WI) European Office
Wilhelm Leuschnerstr. 10
D-60329 Frankfurt/Main
Tel : (49) (69) 23-05-71
Fax : (49) (69) 23-05-93
E-mail: wiscon@ibm.net
Mr John D. Gatto, Director
Ms Mary Donnigan, Trade Specialist

One (1) state, the State of Louisiana, is based in Herborn, Germany:

State of Louisiana (LA) European Office
MLM & Associates
c/o Louisiana Dept. of Economic Development
Sperlingsweg 6
D-35745 Herborn
Tel : (49) (2772) 95-77-10
Fax : (49) (2772) 95-77-11
E-mail: myatt@online.de
Mr M. L. Myatt, Director

One (1) state, the State of Arizona, is based in Munich, Germany:

State of Arizona (AZ) Munich Office
Dietlingerstr. 15
D-80802 Munich
Tel : (49) (89) 36-18-333
Fax : (49) (89) 36-17-094
E-mail: azeurope@compuserve.com
Mr Kristian J. Schnack, Director
Ms Frauke Lindemann, Marketing Executive

One (1) state, the State of Alabama, is based in Stuttgart, Germany:

State of Alabama (AL) European Office
Charlottenplatz 17
D-70173 Stuttgart
Tel : (49) (711) 22-65-604
Fax : (49) (711) 22-65-628
Mr Kurt H. Marshall, Director

US STATE REPRESENTED IN HUNGARY

State of Illinois (IL) - Hungary Office
Rakoczi ut 1-3, Islas Centre
H-1088 Budapest
Tel : (36) (1) 26-65-140
Fax : (36) (1) 26-69-661
E-mail: 100324.2600@compuserve.com
Ms Magda Kertesz, Manager

US STATE REPRESENTED IN ISRAEL

State of Ohio (OH) Eastern Mediterranean Office
110 Hahashmoniam St., P.O. Box 20286
61202 Tel Aviv, Israel
Tel : (972) (35) 62-77-05
Fax : (972) (35) 61-16-11
E-mail: atidedi@netvision.net.il
Mr Richard Schottenstein, Managing Director

US STATE REPRESENTED
IN THE NETHERLANDS

State of Indiana (IN)
WTC Amsterdam, Strawinskylaan 305
NL. 1077 XX Amsterdam
Tel : (31) (20) 57-11-886
Fax : (31) (20) 57-11-889
E-mail: indynl@4all.nl
Mr Jim Sitko, Director
Ms Jennifer Nevins, Trade Specialist

US STATE REPRESENTED IN POLAND

State of Illinois (IL) Poland Office
Chmielna 8, Room 10
PL - 00950 Warsaw
Tel : (48) (22) 82-75-961
Fax : (48) (22) 82-77-089
E-mail: illinois@it.comp.pl
Mr Maciej Cybulski, Manager

US STATE REPRESENTED IN SPAIN

The Commonwealth of Puerto Rico is represented in Spain:

Commonwealth of Puerto Rico
Economic Development
Calle Serrano 1, 21zq
E-28001 Madrid
Tel : (34) (1) 578-0091
Fax : (34) (1) 577-5260
Mr Carlos Rivera Mendoza, Director

also:

Puerto Rico Industrial Development Company
P.O. Box 362350
San Juan, PR 00936-2350
Tel : (1) (787)758-4747
Fax : (1) (787)753-6874

US STATES REPRESENTED IN THE UNITED KINGDOM

Eleven (11) states are represented in the United Kingdom. All are based in London:

State of Arizona (AZ) European Office
116 London Road
GB- Kingston upon Thames KT2 6QJ
Tel : (44) (181) 546-4425
Fax : (44) (181) 546-5526
E-mail: azeurope@compuserve.com
Mr Kristian J. Schnack, Director
Mr H. Grattan Donnelly, Deputy Director

State of California (CA) London Office
27 Dover Street, 2nd Floor
GB - London W1X3PA
Tel : (44) (171) 629-8211
Fax : (44) (171) 629-8223
E-mail: 101354.2700@compuserve.com
Mr Charles Nelson, Investment Director
Ms Beatrice Bouju, Trade Manager

State of Colorado (CO) European Office
Mellier House, 4th Floor
26a Albemarle Street
GB - London W1X 3FA
Tel : (44) (171) 499-7795
Fax : (44) (171) 499-7769
Ms Ellen Emerson, European Representative

State of Florida (FL) London Office
18-24 Westbourne Grove, 1st Floor
GB - London W2 5RH
Tel : (44) (171) 630-91-66
Fax : (44) (171) 630-14-33
Mr Mark E. Diaz, Director
Ms Elizabeth Lizas, Marketing and Trade Specialist

State of Massachusetts (MA) London Office
41 Dover Street
GB - London W1X 3RB
Tel : (44) (171) 495-1978
Fax : (44) (171) 409-3053
Mr Blair Gibb, Director
Mr Francis Pope, Trade Specialist
Mr Zoe McQuillin, Marketing and Trade Specialist

State of Michigan (MI) London Office
110 St Martin's Lane
GB - London WC2N 4DA
Tel : (44) (171) 559-5293
Fax : (44) (171) 240-2470
Ms Ciara McLoughlin, Business Development Manager

State of Mississippi (MS) European Office
1 Northumberland Avenue
Trafalgar Square
GB - London WC2N 5BW
Tel : (44) (171) 872-5608
Fax : (44) (171) 753-2763
Mr Brian Dogherty, Director
Mr Richard Symes, Trade Manager

State or Missouri (MO)
1 Battersea Church Road
GB - London SW 11 3LY
Tel : (44) (171) 771-7017
Fax : (44) (171) 771-7028
E-mail: irp@cibgrp.demon.co.uk
Mr Ian Parker, Director

State of New Jersey (NJ) European Office
95A Chancery Lane, First Floor
GB - London WC2A 1DT
Tel : (44) (171) 404-3703/4
Fax : (44) (171) 404-3698
Ms Gloria Coats, Director

State of New York (NY) London Office
Panton House, 25 Haymarket
GB - London SW1Y 4EN
Tel : (44) (171) 839-5079
Fax : (44) (171) 839-5401
Mr Richard J. Kilner, Director Europe
Mr Martin Lewis, Director Europe Trade Promotion

State of Pennsylvania (PA) London Office
Suite 303, Garden Studios, 11-15 Betterton Street
Covent Garden
GB - London WC2H 9HP
Tel : (44) (171) 470-8818
Fax : (44) (171) 470-8810
E-mail: ap.foreman@easynet.co.uk
Mr Andrew P. Foreman, Director

SUMMARY OF US STATES' PRESENCE IN EUROPE

Total number of states represented: 30 (including Puerto Rico):

Alabama	Minnesota
Arizona	Mississippi
Arkansas	Missouri
California	New Jersey
Colorado	New York
Florida	North Carolina
Georgia	Ohio
Illinois	Oklahoma
Indiana	Pennsylvania
Iowa	Puerto Rico
Kansas	South Carolina
Kentucky	Utah
Louisiana	Virginia
Massachusetts	Washington
Michigan	Wisconsin

Breakdown by countries and cities:

Belgium - 10 states represented:

- Antwerpen - Oklahoma
- Brussels - Arkansas, Georgia, Illinois, Kansas, Kentucky, Michigan, Minnesota, Ohio, Utah

France - 1 state represented

- Paris - Washington

Germany - 15 states represented

- Berlin - Massachusetts
- Cologne - Michigan
- Düsseldorf - North Carolina, Missouri
- Frankfurt/Main - California, Florida, Iowa, New York, Pennsylvania, South Carolina, Virginia, Wisconsin

- Herborn - Louisiana
- Munich - Arizona
- Stuttgart - Alabama

Hungary - 1 state represented:

- Budapest - Illinois

Israel - 1 state represented:

- Tel Aviv - Ohio

Netherlands - 1 state represented:

- Amsterdam - Indiana

Poland - 1 state represented:

- Warsaw - Illinois

Spain - 1 state represented:

- Madrid - Puerto Rico

United Kingdom - 11 states represented:

- London - Arizona, California, Colorado, Florida, Massachusetts, Michigan, Mississippi, Missouri, New Jersey, New York, Pennsylvania

US States not represented in Europe:

Alaska
Connecticut
Delaware
Hawaii
Idaho
Maine
Maryland
Montana
Nebraska
Nevada
New Hampshire

New Mexico
North Dakota
Oregon
Rhode Island
South Dakota
Tennessee
Texas
Vermont
West Virginia
Wyoming

US PORTS

Representation in Belgium

Port Authority of New York and New Jersey
Lange Repeldreef
B-2970 Schilde/Antwerp
Tel : (32) (2) 385-1509
Fax : (32) (2) 385-1510
E-mail: 100432,3360@compuserve.com
Mr J. Ummo Bruns, Director Business Development

Delaware River Port Authority
Braderijstraat 7, bus 4
B-2000 Antwerp
Tel : (32) (3) 234-3960
Tlx : 73460
Fax : (32) (3) 234-3966
Mr R. D. Ludmann, Director

Virginia State Port Authority
Avenue Louise 479, bte 55
B-1050 Brussels
Tel : (32) (2) 648-8072
Fax : (32) (2) 646-3554
Ms Betty J. Princen, Director Marketing Europe

Illinois, Chicago Port Authority
Boulevard de la Cambre 28-30, bte 2
B-1050 Brussels
Tel : (32) (2) 646-5730
Fax : (32) (2) 646-5511
Mr Bart A. Smit, Managing Director

Representation in Germany:

South Carolina, Port of Charleston European Office
International Business Development
Wilhelm-Leuschner Strasse 9-11
D-60329 Frankfurt/Main
Tel : (49) (69) 23-40-71
Fax : (49) (69) 23-40-73
Mr Harley Powell, Director

Representation in Norway:

Georgia Ports Authority
Haakon VII's Gate 5b
P.O. Box 1372
N-0114 Oslo 1
Tel : (47) (2) 83-34-25/6
Fax : (47) (2) 83-16-07
Mr Arthur Rondan, Director Europe

Representation in the United Kingdom:

Maryland Port Administration, Port of Baltimore
Carolyn House, Dingwall Road
GB - Croydon CRO 3ET
Tel : (44) (171) 681-1918/9
Fax : (44) (171) 681-5645
Mr Douglas H. Dickerson, Director

Massachusetts Port Authority
Ivory Gate
41 Dover Street
GB - London W1X 3RB
Tel : (44) (171) 495-1978
Fax : (44) (171) 409-3053
Ms Connie Irwin, Director

Port Authority of New York and New Jersey
Sackville House
40 Piccadilly
GB - London W1V 9PA
Tel : (44) (171) 439-0020
Fax : (44) (171) 439-0040
E-mail: 101354,2621@compuserve.com
Mr P. Zantal, Managing Director

US Regional and City Representatives

Atlanta Economic Corporation
European Office
58 Lange Voorhout
NL - 2514 EG The Hague
Tel : (31) (70) 364-9552
Fax : (31) (70) 365-6297
Mr Philip A. C. Brink, Director

Maryville, Tennessee
Ken Geddes Associates Ltd.
Linden House, 34 Moorgate Road
GB - Rotherham, S60 2AG SouthYorkshire
Tel : (44) (709) 37-51-84
Fax : (44) (709) 37-93-67
Mr R. H. Whiteley, Managing Director

Mississippi Gulf Coast
Harrison County Dev.Commission
Postfach 1424
D-8670 Hof
Tel : (49) (9281) 84526
Mr Reinhardt Frecot, Director

Northeast Pennsylvania
MRC Management Research & Consulting AG
Greifengasse 36, P. O. Box
CH-4058 Basel
Tel : (41) (61) 691-79-55
Fax : (41) (61) 691-70-22
Herrn U. Hardmeier, Director

Sacto Sacramento, California
Sacramento Area Commerce and Trade Organization
P. O. Box 238
CH-1211 Geneva 19, Switzerland
Tel : (41) (22) 734-73-59
Fax : (41) (22) 734-73-58
Mr Milo L. Cermak, Managing Director

US State industrial development organizations assuring liaison with US State representations in Europe.

Alabama
International Development Division
Alabama Development Office
401 Adams Avenue
Montgomery, AL 36104
Tel : (1) (334) 242-0400
Fax : (1) (334) 242-5669
Ira Silbermann, Director
Liaison with State of Alabama Office in Stuttgart/Germany

Alaska
Division of Trade and Development
P. O. Box 110804
Juneau, AK 99811-0804
Tel : (1) (907) 465-2017
Fax : (1) (907) 465-3767
Tom Lawson, Director
No representation of the State of Alaska in Europe

Arizona
Arizona Department of Commerce
3800 N. Central Avenue # 1500
Phoenix, AZ 85012
Tel : (1) (602) 280-1300
Fax : (1) (602) 280-1305
Dave Guthrie, Deputy Director
Liaison with State of Arizona Offices in London/England, and Munich/Germany.

Arkansas
Arkansas Industrial Development Commission
International Marketing
One State Capitol Mall
Little Rock, AR 72201
Tel : (1) (501) 682-7781
Fax : (1) (501) 324-9856
Lauren McDonald, Director
Liaison with State of Arkansas in Brussels/Belgium

California
California Trade & Commerce Agency
Direction of Government & Economic Development
801 K Street, Suite 1926
Sacramento, CA 95814
Tel : (1) (916) 324-9777
Fax : (1) (916) 324-5791
Brenda M. Lopes, Executive Director
Liaison with State of California Office in Frankfurt/Germany and London/England

Colorado
Colorado Office of Business Development
1625 Broadway, Suite 1710
Denver, CO 80202
Tel : (1) (303) 892-3840
Fax : (1) (303) 892-3848
John C. Dill, Director of Economic Development Program
Liaison with State of Colorado Office in London/England.

Connecticut
Connecticut Department of Community Development
505 Hudson Street
Hartford, CT 06106
Tel : (1) (203) 566-3152
Fax : (1) (203) 566-8600
Peter Ellif, Commissioner
No representation of the State of Connecticut in Europe

Delaware
Delaware Economic Development Office
99 Kings Highway
P. O. Box 1401
Dover, DE 19903
Tel : (1) (302) 739-4271
Fax : (1) (302) 739-5749/577-3156
Robert W. Coy Jr, Director
No representation of the State of Delaware in Europe

District of Columbia
Business Services & Economic Development
441 4th Street NW, Suite 1140
Washington DC. 20001
Tel : (1) (202) 727-6365
Fax : (1) (202) 727-6703
W. Davis Watts, Economic Development Director
No representation of the District of Columbia in Europe

Florida
Enterprise Florida
Atrium Building, Suite 201
325 John Knox Road
Tallahassee, FL 32303
Tel : (1) (904) 488-6300
Fax : (1) (904) 922-9595
Stephen Mayberry, Vice-President
Liaison with the State of Florida Office in Frankfurt/Germany, and London/England.

Georgia
Georgia Department of Industry, Trade and Tourism
285 Peachtree Center Avenue, NE
Marquis Tower II, Suite 1100
Atlanta, GA 30303
Tel : (1) (404) 656-3556
Fax : (1) (404) 656-3567
Randolph B. Cardoza, Commissioner
Liaison with State of Georgia Office in Brussels/Belgium

Hawaii
Industry Development Branch Department of Business, Economic
Development and Tourism
P. O. Box 2359
Honolulu, HI 96804
Tel : (1) (808) 586-2355
Fax : (1) (808) 586-2377
Seiji Naya, Director
No representation of the State of Hawaii in Europe

Idaho
Idaho State Department of Commerce
700 West State Street, 2nd Floor
P. O. Box 83720-2700
Boise, ID 83720
Jay Engstrom, Administration for Division of Economic Development
No representation of the State of Idaho in Europe

Illinois
Illinois Department of Commerce
620 E. Adams
Springfield, IL 62701
Tel : (1) (217) 782-7500
Fax : (1) (217) 785-6328
Dennis Whetstone, Director
Liaison with the State of Illinois Office in Brussels/Belgium, Budapest/Hungary
and Warsaw/Poland

Indiana
Business Development Division
Indiana Department of Commerce
One North Capital, Suite 700
Indianapolis, IN 46204-2288
Tel : (1) (317) 232-8800
Fax : (1) (317) 232-4146
David Perlini, Executive Director
Liaison with the State of Indiana Office in Amsterdam/Netherlands

Iowa
Iowa Department of Economic Development
200 East Grand Avenue
Des Moines, IA 50309
Tel : (1) (515) 242-4700
Fax : (1) (515) 242-4749
David Lions, Director
Liaison with the State of Iowa Office in Frankfurt/Germany

Kansas
Kansas Department of Commerce & Housing
700 S. W. Harrison, Suite 1300
Topeka, KS 66603
Tel : (1) (913) 296-5298
Fax : (1) (913) 296-3490
Steve Kelly, Director of Business Development
Liaison with the State of Kansas Office in Brussels/Belgium

Kentucky
Kentucky Cabinet for Economic Development
Capital Plaza Tower, 24th Floor
500 Mero Street
Frankfort, KY 40601-1975
Tel : (1) (502) 564-7670
Fax : (1) (502) 564-7697
Gene Strong, Secretary
Liaison with the State of Kentucky Office in Brussels/Belgium

Louisiana
Louisiana Department of Economic Development
101 France Street
P. O. Box 94185
Baton Rouge, LA 70804
Tel : (1) (504) 342-5361
Fax : (1) (504) 342-5389
Harold Price, Assistant Secretary
Liaison with the State of Louisiana Office in Herborn/Germany

Maine
Maine Department of Economic and Community Development
33 Stone Street
59 State House Station
Augusta, ME 04333-059
Tel : (1) (207) 287-2656
Fax : (1) (207) 287-2861
Thomas Mc Brierty, Commissioner
No representation of the State of Maine in Europe

Maryland
Maryland Office of International Business, 13th Floor
217 E. Reduced Street
Baltimore, MD 21202
Tel : (1) (401) 767-0695
Fax : (1) (401) 333-8200
No representation of the State of Maryland in Europe

Massachusetts
Massachusetts Office of Business Development
One Ashburton Pl. # 2101
Boston, MA 02108
Tel : (1) (617) 727-3206
Fax : (1) (617) 727-8797
Liaison with the State of Massachusetts in London/England and
Berlin/Germany

Michigan
Department of Consumer & Industry Services
P. O. Box 30004
Lansing, MI 48909
Tel : (1) (517) 373-1820
Fax : (1) (517) 373-3872
Liaison with the State of Michigan Office in London/England and Cologne/Germany

Minnesota
State of Minnesota Department of Trade & Economic Development
500 Metro Square
121 7th PL. E
St Paul, Minnesota 55101-2146
Tel : (1) (612) 297-1291
Fax : (1) (612) 296-4772
No formal representation of the State of Minnesota in Europe (c/o Oppenheimer, Wolff & Donnelly - Law Firm, Brussels/Belgium)

Mississippi
Department of Economic and Community Development
P. O. Box 849
Jackson, MS 39205
Tel : (1) (601) 359-3449
Fax : (1) (601) 359-2832
Jimmy Heidel, Executive Director
Liaison with the State of Mississippi in London/England

Missouri
State of Missouri Department of Economic Development
P. O. Box 1157
Jefferson City, MO 65102
Tel : (1) (573) 751-2133
Fax : (1) (573) 751-7384
Jo. Driskill, Director
Liaison with the State of Missouri Office in London/England

Montana
SBA District Office
301 S.Park, Room 334
Helena, MT 65102
Tel : (1) (406) 441-1081
Fax : (1) (406) 441-1090
Jo Alice Mospan, District Director
No representation of the State of Montana in Europe

Nebraska
Nebraska Department of Economic Development
P.O. Box 94666
301 Centennial Mall South
Lincoln, NE 68509-4666
Tel : (1) (402) 471-3111
Fax : (1) (402) 471-3778
Maxine B. Moul, Director
No representation of the State of Nebraska in Europe

Nevada
Nevada Commission of Economic Development
5151 S. Carson Street
Carson City, NV 89710
Tel : (1) (702) 687-4325
Fax : (1) (702) 687-4450
Robert E. Shriver, Executive Director
No representation of the State of Nevada in Europe

New Hampshire
State Office of Industrial Development
P. O. Box 1856
Concord, NH 03302-1856
Tel : (1) (603) 271-2591
Fax : (1) (603) 271-6784
William Pillsbury Jr, Director
No representation of the State of New Hampshire in Europe

New Jersey
New Jersey Department of Commerce and Economic Development
20 W. State Street, 8th Floor, CN 823
Trenton, NJ 08625-0823
Tel : (1) (609) 292-7757
Fax : (1) (609) 777-3106
Cy Thanikary, Director of Economic Development
Liaison with the State of New Jersey in London

New Mexico
Economic Development Department
Joseph M. Montoya Building
1100 St Francis Drive
P. O. Box 20003
Santa Fe , NM 87504-5003
Tel : (1) (505) 827-0381
Fax : (1) (505) 827-0328
Gary D. Bratcher, Cabinet Secretary
No representation of the State of New Mexico in Europe

New York
NY State Department of Economic Development
One Commerce Plaza
Albany, NY 12245
Tel : (1) (518) 474-4100
Fax : (1) (518) 473-9374
Charles A. Gargano, Commissioner
Liaison with the State of New York Office in London/England and
Frankfurt/Germany

North Carolina
International Division
North Carolina Department of Commerce
P. O. Box 29571
Raleigh NC 27626-0571
Tel : (1) (919) 733-4151
Fax : (1) (919) 733-9265
Gary Carlton, Director Business, Industrial Development Division
Liaison with the State of North Carolina Office in Düsseldorf/Germany

Ohio
Ohio Department of Development
77 S High Street, 28th Floor
Columbus, OH 43215-6108
Tel : (1) (614) 466-4551
Fax : (1) (614) 644-1789
Jean C. Ryan, Deputy Director
Liaison with the State of Ohio Office in Brussels/Belgium

Oklahoma
International Trade and Investment Division
Oklahoma Department of Commerce
P. O. Box 26980
Oklahoma City, OK 73126-0980
Tel : (1) (405) 815-6552
Fax : (1) (405) 815-5199
Dr Leo Presley, Executive Director
Liaison with the Oklahoma State Office in Antwerpen/Belgium

Oregon
Oregon Department of Economic Development
775 Summer Street N.E.
Salem, OR 97310
Tel : (1) (503) 986-0256
Fax : (1) (503) 581-5115
William C. Scott, Director
No representation of the State of Oregon in Europe

Pennsylvania
Governor's Action Team
Office of International Trade
Room 439, Forum Building
Harrisburg, PA 17120
Tel : (1) (717) 787-8199
Fax : (1) (717) 772-5419
Steve Kohler, Director
Liaison with the State of Pennsylvania Office in Frankfurt/Germany and
London/England

Puerto Rico
Puerto Rico Industrial Development Administration
G. P. O. Box 362350
San Juan, P. R. 00936-2350
Tel : (1) (787) 758-4747
Fax : (1) (787) 753-6874
Jamie Morgan Stubbe, Administrator
Liaison with the Commonwealth of Puerto Rico Office in Madrid/Spain

Rhode Island
Rhode Island Department of Economic Development
One West Exchange Street
Providence, RI 02903
Tel : (1) (401) 277-2601
Fax : (1) (401) 277-2102
Marcel Valois, Director
No representation of the State of Rhode Island in Europe

South Carolina
South Carolina Department of Commerce
P. O. Box 927
1201 Main Street, 16th Floor
Columbia, SC 29202
Tel : (1) (803) 737-0400
Fax : (1) (803) 737-0418
Robert V. Royall Jr
Liaison with the State of South Carolina Office in Frankfurt/Germany

South Dakota
Governor's Office of Economic Development
Capitol Lake Plaza
711 East Wells Avenue
Pierre, SD 57501-3369
Tel : (1) (605) 773-5032
Fax : (1) (605) 773-5698
Ron Wheeler, Commissioner
No representation of the State of South Dakota in Europe

Tennessee
Tennessee Economic Development Department
Rachel Jackson Building, 8th Floor
320 6th Avenue North
Nashville, TN 37243-0405
Tel : (1) (615) 741-1888
Fax : (1) (615) 741-7306
William A. Dunavant Jr, Commissioner
No representation of the State of Tennessee in Europe

Texas
Texas Department of Economic Development
1700 N. Congress
P. O. Box 12728
Austin, TX 78711-2728
Tel : (1) (512) 936-0101
Fax : (1) (512) 936-0303
No representation of the State of Texas in Europe

Utah
Utah Division of Business and Economic Development
324 S. State Street, Suite 500
Salt Lake City, Utah 84111
Tel : (1) (801) 538-8800
Fax : (1) (801) 538-8889
Dan Mabey, Director International Development
Liaison with the State of Utah Benelux Office in Brussels/Belgium

Vermont
SBA District Office
87 State Street
P. O. Box 605
Montpelier, VT 05601-0605
Tel : (1) (802) 828-4422
Fax : (1) (802) 828-4485
Kenneth Silvia, District Director
No representation of the State of Vermont in Europe

Virginia
Department of Economic Development
901 East Byrd Street
P. O. Box 798
Richmond, VA 23218-0798
Tel : (1) (804) 371-8106
Fax : (1) (804) 371-8112
Wayne L. Stirling, Executive Director
Liaison with the State of Virginia Office in Frankfurt/Germany

Washington
State Department of Community, Trade & Economic Development
906 Columbia Street S.W.
P. O. Box 48300
Olympia WA 98504-8300
Tel : (1) (360) 753-7426
Fax : (1) (360) 586-3582
Tim Douglas, Director
Liaison with the State of Washington Office in Paris/France

West Virginia
West Virginia Economic Development Authority
1018 Kanawha Boulevard E., # 501
Charleston, WV 25301-2827
Tel : (1) (304) 558-3650
Fax : (1) (304) 558-0206
David Warner, Executive Director
No representation of the State of West Virginia in Europe

Wisconsin
Wisconsin Department of Development
123 W. Washington Avenue
P. O. Box 7970
Madison, WI 53707
Tel : (1) 608) 266-1018
Fax : (1) (608) 267-0436
Bill Mc Coshen, Secretary of Commerce
Liaison with the State of Wisconsin in Germany

Wyoming
Wyoming Economic & Commercial Development Division
Herscher Building
122 W. 25th Street
Cheyenne, WY 82202
Tel : (1) (307) 777-7284
Fax : (1) (307) 777-5840
Vivian Watkins, Director
No representation of the State of Wyoming in Europe

CHAPTER 9
US CONSULTANTS
SPECIALIZING IN EU MATTERS

The need for information, advice and a voice in Brussels is often met by companies by taking on the services of a Consultant. Consultants come from a variety of backgrounds. Most EU Affairs Consultants are drawn from the ranks of economists, political scientists, journalists, lawyers, accountants and public relations executives.

Besides the advice they can provide on what the institutions are doing and how to benefit from their activities, they are increasingly advising their clients on how they can actually influence the decision-making process.

Brussels abounds with Consultants, Management Consultants, Public Affairs Advisors, Public Relations Firms, Regulatory Advocates, Lawyers etc..

This Chapter provides the names of US Consultants specializing in EU matters:

■ **APCO Associates Inc.**
1615 L. Street N.W. - Suite 900
Washington DC. 20036
Tel : (1) (202) 466-6002
Fax : (1) (202) 778-1000
Contact : M. Kraus

Avenue Louise 250, Bte 52
B - 1080 Brussels
Tel : (32) (2) 626-0070
Fax : (32) (2) 626-0075
E-mail: m.dober@netropolis.be/76734.2462@compuserve.com
Contact : M. Dober
PoliticalC onsultants
Founded: April 1st, 1995
Number of Consultants: 6
Specialization: Food Products and Beverages
                    Information Technology
                    Intellectual Property

■ **Edelman Public Relations Worldwide**
US HQ-1500 Broadway
New-York, NY 10036
Tel : (1) (212) 768-0550
Fax : (1) (212) 704-0128

Edelman Europe Brussels
Avenue de Tervuren 13a
B - 1040 Brussels
Tel : (32) (2) 732-2600
Fax : (32) (2) 732-2076
Contact : A. Byrne
Political and Public Relations Consultants
Founded in: 1954: (USA) - 1970 (Europe)
Number of Consultants in Europe: 300
Relations with all the Directorates General of the European Commission
Specialization: All sectors

■ **Hartman Whyte International Corporation**
56 Arbor Street
Harford, CT 06106
Tel : (1) (203) 233-1079
Tel : (1) (203) 233-4057
Fax : (1) (203) 232-4749
Contact : B. Hartman Tucker
          M. Whyte
Founded in 1988
Number of Consultants: 7
Specialization: Information and Specific Consulting on EU
                    Eastern Europe with Small and Medium-Sized American
                    and European companies, as well as Financing of Joint
                    Companies
                    Import/Export Services
                    Eastern Europe and the EU
                    Information Service and Information Agency

■ **International Technology and Trade Associates Inc. ITTA**
1330 Connecticut Avenue NW, Suite 210
Washington DC 20036
Tel : (1) (202) 828-8614
Fax : (1) (202) 828-2617
Contact : C. W. Dyke
        M. J. Sierra

Avenue Louise 65, Bte 11
B - 1050 Brussels
Tel : (32) (2) 535-7898
Fax : (32) (2) 535-7700
Contact : J. L. Sollinger
Founded November 27, 1989
Number of Consultants: 12
Relations with the Directorates General of the Commission I, IA, III - External
Economic Relations, External Political Relations, Industry
Specialization: Commerce
                    Technology
                    Investments
                    Public Affairs

■ **Strategic Analysis Inc.**
Fairlane Road 11
Reading, PA 19106
Tel : (1) (215) 779-9080
Fax : (1) (215) 779-1761

Strategic Analysis Europe
Avenue Louise 66
B - 1050 Brussels
Tel : (32) (2) 512-3020
Fax : (32) (2) 513-1726
Contact :   F. Nordhoy
          E. Nordhoy
Management Consultants
Founded in 1984
Number of Consultants: 12

CHAPTER 10
OTHER CONSULTANTS SPECIALIZED IN EU MATTERS WITH AFFILIATES IN THE US

Among the other consultants specialized in EU matters, you will note the presence of major US Accounting Firms.

US Accounting Firms have developed operations to meet the need for EU-related advice. Their aim is to offer clients "one-stop-shopping", providing them with a "multi-disciplinary approach" to advice that encompasses legal, managerial and marketing/aspects.

Two different approaches have been taken by accountancy firms in the area of EU monitoring and lobbying. Some, like KPMG, retain the services of a Brussels Law Firm to advise their EU-Centre. Others like DRT International (Deloitte's/Touche Ross),employ lawyers and consultants in their EU operation, and only seek opinions from independent counsel in certain situations.

Many of these firms provide free informational documents explaining the structure and functioning of the European institutions, as well as updates on legislative developments. Some of the firms maintain databases on EU developments which are updated regularly.

■ **Arthur D. Little**
Bd de la Woluwe, 2
B - 1150 Brussels
Tel : (32) (2) 762-0285
Fax : (32) (2) 762-0758
Contact: Van Ranst
Management Consultants
Founded in 1966
Number of Consultants: 60

Specialization: Strategy and Organization
Management of Change
Management of Technology
Information Technology
Operations
Environment and Security
All Industrial, Financial and Commercial Sectors

HQ in Cambridge (MA) USA

■ **Bossard Consultants**
Avenue de la Joyeuse Entrée, 1
B - 1040 Brussels
Tel : (32) (2) 285-0028
Fax : (32) (2) 285-0033
Contact: P. Bradstreet
Management Consultants
Founded September 1st, 1984
Number of Consultants: 4

Office in the USA:
22 Putnam Avenue
Cambridge MA 02139
Tel : (1) (617) 354-2320
Fax : (1) (617) 576-1362

■ **Burson-Marsteller S.A.**
Avenue Louise, 22 5
B - 1050 Brussels
Tel : (32) (2) 626-0640
Fax : (32) (2) 647-9530
E-mail: bm.brussels@bm.com
Contact: J. Ral
Political and PR Consultants
Founded 1961
Number of Consultants: 11
Specialization: Public Affairs, Public Relations, Communication

■ **Cesemaan S.A.**
Tour Louise
Avenue Louise 149, Bte 18
B - 1050 Brussels
Tel : (32) (2) 542-0600
Fax : (32) (2) 542-0649
Contact: B. Brighi
Political Consultants
Founded April 5, 1989
Number of Consultants: 8
Specialization: Transportation
                Agriculture
                Environment
                Public Health
                Professional Training
                Cooperation in the Third Countries

Office in USA:
C. T. USA Inc.
324 East 41st Street
Suite 902
New York. NY 10017
Tel : (1) (212) 490-3115
Fax : (1) (212) 490-3217
Contact: R. Facchinetti

■ **Consultancy Europe Associates Ltd**
(incorporating Spicers Centre for Europe)
Square Marie-Louise, 49
B - 1000 Brussels
Contact: C. Ashby
Political Consultants:
Founded in 1990
Number of Consultants: 10

Specialization: Regulation Law EU
                     Parliament
                     Commission
                     Court of Justice
                     Councils
                     Official Documents of the EU
                     Seminars
                     Budgets
                     Cohesion Funds
                     Structural Funds

Office in the USA:
c/o 414 22nd Street NW
Washington DC.20037
Tel : (1) (202) 887-8500
Fax : (1) (202) 728-1863
Contact: E. Hauck

■Coopers & Lybrand Europe S.A.
European Union Office
Avenue de Tervuren, 2
B - 1040 Brussels
Tel : (32) (2) 741-0811
Fax : (32) (2) 733-6618
E-mail: colybrand.com
Contact: F. Mc Fadden
Management Consultants
Founded in 1990
Number of Consultants: over 30
Specialization: Coopers & Lybrand Europe EU Office is one of the top
consulting firms in Brussels. Specialized in European
Affairs, it serves as consultant to the European Commission,
National Governments as well as public and private
companies throughout the world.
Community and Pan-European subjects
Information Services and Community Publications

■ Deloitte & Touche Europe Services

Rue Archimède, 17
B - 1000 Brussels
Tel : (32) (2) 282-0333
Fax : (32) (2) 282-0310
E-mail:dtt.be.brussels
Contact: R. Doherty
Contact: G. Branton
Founded in 1988
Number of Consultants: 12
Specialization: Deloitte & Touche Europe Service belongs to Deloitte Touche Tohmatsu International and includes 56,000 persons in over 100 countries. The Deloitte & Touche Services Office is responsible for all contacts between the group and the Community Institutions. It has multidisciplinary knowledge concerning EU Affairs, available to its clients throughout the world.

These services include: Entrance Strategy in the Single Market
Investment Advice in Eastern Europe
EU Legislation Monitoring Service
Financial Assistance and Subsidies
Regional Planning Development and use of Public Subsidies
Studies on the formation of companies in countries of Western and Eastern Europe
Commercial EU Legislation and Customs Procedures including Anti-dumping procedures.
Awareness Programs in the European Legal Area
Public Affairs Counsels to influence EU Legislation

■ Ernst & Young European Union Office

Avenue Marcel Thiry, 204
B - 1200 Brussels
Tel : (32) (2) 774-9621
Fax : (32) (2) 774-9628
Political Consultants
Founded: January 1, 1995
Number of Consultants: 2
Specialization: Information on Legal European Developments and Others
Studies for the European Institutions

■ **ESL & Network Europe**
rue de la Loi, 81A
B - 1040 Brussels
Tel : (32) (2) 230-5629
Fax : (32) (2) 230-5319
Contact: Cagneux
Political and Management Consultant
Founded in 1989
Number of Consultants: 70 and 100 Associates
Specialization: Social Affairs and Management Strategy
                   Transportation and Telecommunications
                   Financial Affairs and Environment

Office in the USA:
SGA
1133 Connecticut Avenue NW
Washington DC 20063
Tel : (1) (202) 223-4001
Fax : (1) (202) 457-6566
Contact: S. Agger

■ **European Document Research**
Rue de Trèves, 61
B - 1040 Brussels
Tel : (32) (2) 230-8814
Fax : (32) (2) 230-8965
E-mail: 72360.514@compuserve.com
Contact: H. J. H. Oosterloo
Political and Public Relations Consultant
Founded in September 1992
Number of Consultants: 2
Specialization: Documentation on EU
                   Laws, Regulations, Projects
                   Compilation of European law

Office in the USA:
1100 17th Street NW
Suite 301
Washington DC 20036
Tel : (1) (202) 785-8494
Fax : (1) (202) 785-8589
E-mail: 72360.513@compuserve.com
Contact: G. Lesser

■ **Hill and Knowlton International Belgium**
Avenue Louise, 430
B - 1050 Brussels
Tel: (32) (2) 640-0495
Fax: (32) (2) 640-5072
E-mail: ecruikshanks@zvl.mhs.compuserve.com
Public Affairs and Public Relations Consultants
Founded in 1967
Number of Consultants: 15 specialized in EU law
Specialization: European Legislation, Monitoring and Analysis Service
                   Communication   Counsels   (Establishment   of
                   Agreements/Lobbying Strategy)
                   Internet Services

■ **Interel**
Boulevard Saint-Michel, 78
B - 1040 Brussels
Tel : (32) (2) 732-1188
Fax : (32) (2) 732-1394
E-mail: Interel@innet.be
Contact: J. L. Schuybroek
Political and Public Relations Consultants
Founded: September 1st, 1983
Number of Consultants: 27

Specialization: Environment
                          Social Affairs
                          Food Products
                          Taxes
                          Sport
                          Air Transportation
                          EU Enlargement
                          Telecommunications
                          Pharmaceutical Products
                          Health

Office in the USA:
1200, 19th Street NW
Washington DC 20036
Tel : (1) (202) 857-1189
Fax : (1) (202) 857-1186
E-mail: steve.worth@sba.com
Contact: S. Worth

■ **KPMG European Headquarters**
Avenue Louise, 54
B - 1050 Brussels
Tel : (32) (2) 548-0911
Fax : (32) (2) 548-0909
Contact: R. Ebling
Contact: S. Maddens
Management Consultants
Legal Implications of EU Developments
Implications of EU Developments on Strategic Planning of Private and Public Sectors Information Service and Analysis of Practical Impact of EU Developments
Specialized Services in the Areas of Competition, Commercial Law and European Customs Law Pan-European Studies

■ **Kreab Europe**
Avenue de Tervuren, 13A
B - 1040 Brussels
Tel : (32) (2) 237-6900
Fax : (32) (2) 737-6940
E-mail: Kreab@kreab.se
Contact: G. Danell
Communication Consultants
Founded in 1992
Number of Consultants: 5 plus 2 Advisors
Specialization: Strategic Advice and Implementation of the Communication
Needs and Activities in: European Public Affairs
                             Internal Communication
                             Public Relations
                             Investors' Reports
                             Communication on the Market
                             Crises Management
                             Events
                             Exhibitions
                             Campaigns

Office in the USA:
Kreab USA
Strategy XXI Group
515 Madison Avenue
New York, N.Y. 10022
Tel : (1) (212) 935-0210
Fax : (1) (212) 935-6577
Contact: H. Mouchly-Weiss

■ Ogilvy Adams & Rinehardt S.A.
Avenue Louise, 489
B - 1050 Brussels
Tel : (32) (2) 629-5580
Fax : (32) (2) 640-8620
E-mail: 100774.27@compuserve.com
Contact: Anderson
Public Relations Consultants
Founded in 1956
Number of Consultants: 12
Specialization: Health, Medicine
                   Banking, Systems of Payment
                   Finance and Value Added Tax (VAT)
                   Public Relations European Coordination
                   Environment
                   Launching of Products on the Market
                   Awareness Campaigns for the Governments of the EU,
                   Eastern Europe

■ Price Waterhouse EU Services S. A.
EU Law Unit
Place St. Lambert ,14
B - 1200 Brussels
Tel : (32) (2) 773-4911
Fax : (32) (2) 762-5100
Contact: A. Gorrie
Contact: M. Picat
Consultants in EU law
Founded in 1988 (Creation of the EU Bureau Service)
Number of Consultants: 10 based in Brussels, plus a network spread throughout Europe

Specialization: Competition Policy
                   Financial Services
                   Corporate European Law
                   Value Added Tax
                   Social Policy
                   Environment
                   International Trade
                   Relations EU-Eastern Europe
                   EU Subsidies (Structural Funds, R & D Programs)
                   Access to other Price Waterhouse Experts in areas such as
                   Mergers and Acquisitions, Corporate Tax Law, Customs,
                   Corporate Strategy

■ PRP - Public Relations Partners
Avenue Vandendriessche, 5
B - 1150 Brussels
Tel : (32) (2) 762-0485
Fax : (32) (2) 771-1959
E-mail: 100645.1706@compuserve.com
Contact: J. Lechat
Political and Public Relations Consultants
Founded in 1963
Number of Consultants: 8
Specialization: Aeronautics
                   Consumers
                   Environment
                   European Public Affairs
                   Information Technology
                   Internal Communication
                   Institutional Communication
                   Crisis Communication

Office in the USA:
KCS & A Public & Investor Relations
820 Second Avenue
New York, N.Y. 10017
Tel : (1) (212) 682-6300
Fax : (1) (212) 697-0910
Contact: L. Schupak

■ **W. S. Atkins International Ltd**
Rue de l'Industrie, 4 - Bte 5
B - 1000 Brussels
Tel : (32) (2) 502-0270
Fax : (32) (2) 512-1225
Contact: L. Platteuw
Management Consultants
Founded in 1938
Specialization: Industrial and Economic Planning
                  Market Studies
                  Industrial and Sectoral Studies, Corporate Studies
                  Information Technology
                  Telecommunications
                  Assurance of Quality Standards
                  Road, Maritime and Air Infrastructure Transportation Planning
                  Regional Development
                  Energy
                  Environmental Impact Studies
                  Water Treatment and Waste Management
                  Health and Security
                  Agriculture
                  Production and Construction Industries
                  Management of Engineering Projects
                  Experience in EU Sectoral Studies

CHAPTER 11
US LAW FIRMS REPRESENTED
IN BRUSSELS

There are 34 American Law Firms that have chosen Brussels as the center of their European practice. The list hereafter is not exhaustive and no discrimination is intended.

Firm's Name	**US HQ**
Akin, Gump, Strauss, Hauer & Feld	Washington, D.C.
Allen & Overy	New York, NY
Baker & Mc Kenzie	Chicago, IL
Broderick Terry R.	US Lawyer
Cleary, Gottlieb, Steen & Hamilton	New York, NY
Coudert Brothers	New York, NY
Covington & Burling	Washington, D.C.
Dechert Price & Rhoads	Philadelphia, PA
Dobson & Pinci	New York, NY
Dorsey & Whitney	Minneapolis, MN
Foley & Lardner	Milwaukee, WI
Hogan & Hartson	Washington, D.C.
Hunton & Williams	Richmond, VA
Jones, Day, Reavis & Pogue	Cleveland, OH
Keller & Heckman	Washington, D.C.
Kelley, Drye and Warren	New York, NY
Kilpatrick Stockton	Atlanta, GA
Le Boeuf, Lamb, Green & Macrae	New York, NY
Mayer, Brown & Platt	Chicago, IL
Mc Guire, Woods, Battle & Boothe	Richmond, VA
Mc Kenna & Cuneo	Washington DC
Morgan, Lewis & Bockius	Philadelphia, PA
Morrison & Foerster	San Francisco, CA
Oppenheimer, Wolff & Donnelly	St Paul, MN
Seyfarm, Shaw, Fairweather & Geraldson	Washington, D.C.
Sher & Associates, Paul D.	US Lawyer
Skadden, Arps, Slate, Meagher & Flom	New York, NY

Squire, Sanders & Dempsey	Cleveland, OH
Stewart & Stewart	Washington, D.C.
Thomson, Hine & Flory	Cleveland, OH
Weil, Gotshal & Manges	New York, NY
White & Case	New York, NY
Wilmer, Cutler & Pickering	Washington DC
Winthrop, Stimson, Putnam & Roberts	New York, NY

The Brussels Office usually handles commercial, regulatory, labor and litigation matters at the European Union and national levels.

The Commercial Practice most often focuses on international business transactions, including mergers and acquisitions, privatizations, project finance, joint-ventures, licensing and distribution and international trade.

The Regulatory Practice usually centers on energy, environmental, occupational health and safety, chemical and pharmaceutical, product standards, intellectual property matters etc. This work encompasses advice concerning specific issues in the context of compliance, permitting and enforcement, as well as advice relating to the impact of certain laws and liabilities on business transactions. American law firms also analyse and draft position papers on EU and national legislative proposals.

The Labor Practice usually includes representation regarding transfer of undertaking, collective dismissals, closings, employment policies and conditions and related tax and social security issues.

Finally, the Ligitation Practice involves administrative. business, contractual, labor and other matters before Belgian and international courts.

Admittedly, lawyers working for American law firms in Brussels are fluent in several EU languages.

The total number of lawyers i.e. working for US law firms and specializing in European Community law approaches 200. Most US law firms represented in Brussels employ only between 5 to 10 Attorneys. Of course, many firms also maintain offices in other European countries that handle specific national matters.

■ **Akin, Gump, Strauss, Hauer & Feld**
UQ HQ - 1333 New Hampshire Avenue NW
Suite 400
Washington DC 20036
Tel : (1) (202) 887-4000
Fax : (1) (202) 887-4288

Akin, Gump, Strauss, Hauer & Feld
Avenue Louise, 65 - Bte 7
B-1050 Brussels
Email : akinbr@compuserve.com
Tel : (32) (2) 535-2911
Fax : (32) (2) 535-2900
Jack Langlois, Managing Partner (as of 01/01/98)
Jacques Bourgeois, Partner
Rufus Yerxa, Partner
Peter Verhaege, Partner
Martine Dewitte, Partner
Alain Dejonge, Lawyer
Daniela Della Rosa, Lawyer
Rony Gerrits, Lawyer
Dimitrios Marantis, Lawyer
Jan Van Besen, Lawyer
#of Attorneys specialised in Community law : 5
Specialty : All areas of European Community Law

■ **Allen & Overy**
US HQ - Swiss Bank Tower
10 East 50th Street, 27th Floor
New York, NY 10020

Allen & Overy
Rue de la Loi, 99 - Bte 8
B-1040 Brussels
Tel : (32) (2) 230-2791
Fax : (32) (2) 230-6613
Michael J. Reynolds, Resident Parner
David M. Harrison, Senior Assistant
Philip Mansfield, Assistant
Colin Overbury, Consultant
# of Attorneys specialized in Community law : 4

■ **Baker & Mc Kenzie**
US HQ - Suite 2500
Presidential Plaza One
130 East Randolph Drive
Chicago, Illinois 60601

Baker & Mc Kenzie
Boulevard du Régent, 40
B-1000 Brussels
Tel : (32) (2) 506-3611
Fax : (32) (2) 511-6280
Luc Hinnekens, Partner
Jacques Ghysbrecht, Partner
Otto Grolig, Partner
Ignace Maes, Partner
Paul Herten, Lawyer
Pierre Sculier, Lawyer
Jozef Slootsman, Lawyer
Dominique Lechien, Lawyer
François Gabriel, Lawyer
Alain Huyghe, Lawyer
Koen Vanhaerents, Lawyer
# of Attorneys specialized in Community law :
Specialty :   All areas, more particularly :
                        - Competition
                        - Public Procurement
                        - Areas which are developing in Communiy law

■ **Broderick Terry R.**
Avenue Louise, 475 - Bte 8
B-1050 Brussels
Tel : (32) (2) 646-0019
Fax : (32) (2) 646-0152
Terry R. Broderick
# of Attorneys specialized in Community law : 1

Specialty :   Company law
Competition
Distribution and Franchising
Development of the Internal Market (including specific industrial sectors)
Intellectual Property and Licences
Mergers, Acquisitions, Joint-Ventures
Commercial law

■ **Cleary, Gottlieb, Steen & Hamilton**
US HQ - One Liberty Plaza
New York - NY 10006

Cleay, Gottlieb, Steen & Hamilton
Rue de la Loi, 23 - Bte 5
B-1040 Brussels
Tel : (32) (2) 287-2000
Fax : (32) (2) 231-1661 & 230-1635
Walter Oberreit, Partner
Mario Siragusa, Partner
Wolfgang Knapp, Partner
Jean-Louis Joris, Partner
George Bustin, Partner
Jan Meyers, Partner
Jacques Reding, Partner
Maurits Dolmans, Partner
Antoine Winckler, Partner
Jay Modrall, Partner
Giuseppe Scassellati, Partner
Roman Subiotto, Partner
Till Mueller-Ibold, Special Counsel
# of Attorneys specialized in Community law :
Specialty :   Anti-dumping and Other Business Matters
Competition
Finance and Insurance

■ **Coudert Brothers**
US HQ - 1114 Avenue of the Americas
New York, NY 10036 - 77794
Tel : (1) (212) 626-4400
Fax : (1) (212) 626-4120

Coudert Brothers
Avenue Louise, 149 - Bte 8
B-1050 Brussels
Tel : (32) (2) 542-1811
Fax : (32) (2) 539-2888 & 537-2710

Jacques Buhart, Partner
Stephen O. Spinks, Partner
Paulette Vander Schueren, Partner
Hervé Cogels, Partner
Jean-Yves Art, Partner
Nathalie Gilson, Lawyer
Dirk Van Liedekerke, Lawyer
Kent S. Karlson, Lawyer
Damien Geradin, Lawyer
David Luff, Lawyer
Lawrence Freeman, Lawyer
José San Bento de Menezes, Consultant
# of Attorneys specialized in Community law : Antitrust - (11)
Anti-Dumping - (8)
Telecommunication - (5)
Trade General - (8)
Environment - (2)

Specialty :   Antitrust
Antidumping
Telecommunications
Trade general
Environment

■ **Covington & Burling**
US HQ - P.O. Box 7566
1201 Pennsylvania Avenue NW
Washington DC 20044
Tel : (1) (202) 662-6000
Fax : (1) (202) 662-6291 & 737-0528
Contact : **J.D. Blake**

Covington & Burling
Avenue des Arts, 44 - Bte 8
B-1040 Brussels
Tel : (32) (2) 549-5230
Fax : (32) (2) 502-1598
Henriette Tielemans, Lawyer
David L. Harfst, Lawyer
# of Attorneys specialized in Community law : 6
Specialty :   Business and Competition Area (Mergers, Joint Companies,
                Exclusive Franchise and Distribution Agreements)
                Environment
                Consumer Law
                Product Liability
                Regulation of Food Products, Pharmaceuticals Products and
                Cosmetics
                Intellectual Property
                Litigation and Arbitration

■ **Dechert, Price & Rhoads**
US HQ - 4000 Bell Atlantic Tower
1717 Arch Street
Philadelphia, PA 19103 - 2793
Tel : (1) (215) 994-4000
Fax : (1) (215) 994-2222
Contact : **S.S. Browne**

Dechert, Price & Rhoads
Avenue Louise, 65 - Bte 4
B-1050 Brussels
Tel : (32) (2) 535-5411
Fax : (32) (2) 535-5400
Richard J. Temko, Partner
Melvin A. Schwarz, Partner
Bernardine Adkins, Associate
George Van Mellaert, Associate
Jean-Pierre Magremanne,Associate
Anne Schollen, Associate
**# of Attorneys specialized in Community law : 3 (Brussels); 5 (London),
2 (Paris), 4 (Philadelphia), 2 (Washington), 2 (New York)**
Specialty :   Competition
            Taxation
            Banking and Finance
            Aviation
            Public Procurement

■**Dobson & Pinci**
US HQ - 645 Madison avenue
New York, NY 10022

Dobson & Pinci
Avenue Franklin Roosevelt, 84
B-1050 Brussels
Tel : (32)(2)647-0700
Fax : (32) (2)647-6440
David M. Dobson, Lawyer
Anthony Sistilli, Lawyer
# of Attorneys specialized in Community Law :
Specialty :

■ **Dorsey & Whitney**
US HQ - 220 South Sixth Street
Minneapolis, MN 55402 - 1498
Tel : (1) (612) 340-2600
Fax : (1) (612) 340-2868
Contact : **T.O. Moe**

Dorsey & Whitney LLP
Square de Meeûs 35
B-1000 Brussels
Tel : (32) (2) 504-4611
Fax : (32) (2) 504-4646
Barry D. Glazer, Partner
Bernd U. Graf, Partner
# of Attorneys specialized in Community law : 2
Specialty :   **Barry D. Glazer** : Competition
                Bernd U. Graf : Competition and Commercial Law

■ **Foley & Lardner**
US HQ - 777 East Wisconsin Avenue
Milwaukee, WI 53202 - 5367
Tel : (1) (414) 271-2400
Fax : (1) (414) 297-4900
Contact : **Ralf R. Böer**

Foley & Lardner
Avenue Louise, 283 - Bte 5
B-1050 Brussels
Tel : (32) (2) 646-2777
Fax : (32) (2) 646-7574
Dr. Daniel Ewert, Brussels
Howard W. Fogt, Brussels, Washington,D.C.
Ilene Knable, Washington, D.C.
Melinda F. Levitt, Washington, D.C.
Robert A. Burka, Washington, D.C.
# of Attorneys specialized in Community law : 5
Specialty :   All Areas of Community law, and International Business Law

■ **Hogan & Hartson**
US HQ - 555 13th Street NW
Washington DC 20004-1109
Tel : (1) (202) 637-5600
Fax : (1) (202) 637-5910
Contact : **B.G. Odle**

Hogan & Hartson
Avenue des Arts , 41
B-1040 Brussels
Tel : (32) (2) 505-0911
Fax : (32) (2) 505-0996
ClaudeV.S. Eley, Partner in charge
Gerald E. Oberst, Partner
Dirk Lontings,   Partner
Guido Lamal, Associate
Lisa Zannoni, Associate
André Logie, Associate
# of Attorneys specialized in Community Law : 5
Specialty :   Food Products, Biotechnology and Agriculture
International Trade
Financial Services
Belgian Law
Telecommunications and Satellites
Pharmaceutical Products
Competition and Commercial Rules
Environment and Security
Industrial and Technical Standards
Public Procurement
State Subsidies
Labor Law
Free Circulation of Persons, Goods and Services
Litigation in front of the Court of Justice and the Tribunal of First
Instance (equivalent to US District Court)
Mergers and Acquisitions
Trade and International Investments
Claude v.S. Eley : Corporate Law, Commercial Law, Mergers
and Acquisitions, Commerce and International Investments
Gerald E. Oberst : Telecommunications and Satellites
Dirk Lontings : Financial Services, Belgian Law, Commercial
Law

Guido Lamal : Labor, Employment, Social Security
Filip Tuytschaever : International Trade, Competition, Environment, Industrial and Technical Standards, Public Procurement, State Subsidies
Lisa Zannoni : Food Products, Biotechnology and Agriculture, Pharmaceutical Products
André Logie : Telecommunications and Satellites

■ **Hunton & Williams**
US HQ - P.O. Box 1535
700 East Main Street
Richmond, VA 23212-1535
Tel : (1) (804) 788-8200
Fax : (1) (804) 788-8218/8219/8669

Hunton & Williams
Avenue Louise, 106
B-1050 Brussels
Tel : (32) (2) 646-0010 & 648-1667 & 648-1754 & 648-1773
Fax: (32) (2) 646-0246
Charles A. Blanchard, Managing Partner
Prof. Lucas Bergamp, Resident Counsel
Roszell Hunter, Resident Partner
Etienne Lehmann, Resident Associate
Frederic Hendricks, Resident Associate
Patrice De Hemptinne, Resident Associate
Jean-Louis Berra, Resident Associate
Koen Muylle, Resident Associate
Katarine C. Baragona, Resident Associate
Nicole Cambre, Resident Associate
# of Attorneys specialized in Community law : 9
Specialty :   Environment
               Health and Safety
               Product Standards Practice
               Chemicals, Pharmaceuticals, Food & Drugs, and Biotechnology
               Energy
               Labor
               Litigation
               Corporate practice

■ **Jones, Day, Reavis & Pogue**
US HQ - North Point
901 Lakeside Avenue
Cleveland, OH 44114
Tel : (1) (216) 586-3939
Fax: (1) (216) 579-0212
Contact : **R. Rawson**

Jones, Day, Reavis & Pogue
Avenue Louise, 480, 7th Floor
ITT Tower
B-1050 Brussels
Tel : (32) (2) 645-1411
Fax: (32) (2) 645-1445
Luc G. Houben, Partner
Thierry Buytaert, Lawyer
Ghislain T. Joseph, Partner
Norbert Koch, Partner
Hendrick Bourgeois, Lawyer

# of Attorneys specialized in Community Law : 5
Specialty :   **Thierry Buytaert** : Banking
                Luc G. Houben : Corporate Law
                Ghislain T. Joseph : Tax Law
                Norbert Koch : Competition, Industrial Property

■ **Keller & Heckman**
US HQ - 1001 G Street NW
Suite 500 West
Washington DC 20001
Tel : (1) (202) 434-4100
Fax : (1) (202) 434-4646
Contact : **J. Eldred**

Keller & Heckman
Boulevard Louis Schmidt, 87
B-1040 Brussels
Tel : (32) (2) 732-5280
Fax: (32) (2) 732-5392
Jean-Philippe Montfort, Lawyer
Jean Savigny, Resident Partner
Alexandre Mencik von Zebinsky, Lawyer
Philippe Andrews, Lawyer
# of Attorneys specialized in Community Law : 4
Specialty :   **Jean Savigny** : Food Products, Antitrust, General
Jean-Philippe Montfort : Food Products; Pharmaceuticals;
Environment
Alexandre Mencik von Zebinsky : Food Products;
Pharmaceuticals, Telecommunications
Philippe Andrews, Food Products, Environment

■ **Kelley, Drye & Warren**
US HQ - 101 Park Avenue
New York, NY 10178
Tel : (1) (212) 808-7800
Fax : (1) (212) 808-7897
Contact : **J. Callagy**

Kelley, Drye & Warren
Avenue Louise, 106 - Bte 7
B-1050 Brussels
Tel : (32) (2) 646-1110
Fax : (32) (2) 640-0589
André Van Landuyt, Partner
# of Attorneys specialized in Community Law : 5
Specialty :   Finance
General Affairs
Community Law in General

■ **Kilpatrick Stockton**
US HQ - 1100 Peachtree Street, Suite 2800
Atlanta, GA 30309-4530
Tel : (1) (404) 815-6500
Fax : (1) (404) 815-6555

Kilpatrick Stockton
Avenue Louise, 149 - Bte 15
B-1050 Brussels
Tel: : (32) (2) 533-0300
Fax : (32) (2) 534-8638
Frederick K. Heller Jr, Managing Partner
Pascale F. Rahman, Counsel
# of Attorneys specialized in Community Law : 2
Specialty :   Telecommunications

■ **Le Boeuf, Lamb, Green & Macrae**
US HQ - 125 West 55th Street
New York, NY 10019 - 5389
Tel : (1) (212) 424-8000
Fax : (1) (212) 424-8500

Le Boeuf, Lamb, Greene & Macrae
Avenue des Arts, 19 H
B-1000 Brussels
Tel : (32) (2) 227-0900
Fax : (32) (2)227-0909
Leonard W.N. Hawkes, Partner
James K. Lockett, Partner
Guy Soussan, Partner
Vernon Vig, Partner
# of Attorneys specialized in Community law : 9
Specialty: Competition
              Commerce and Customs
              Environment
              Telecommunications
              Insurance and Finance
              Public Procurement
              European Economic Space and Eastern Europe
              Energy
              The Four Freedoms of EU and Audiovisual

■ **Mayer, Brown & Platt**
US HQ - 190 South LaSalle Street
Chicago , Illinois 60603-3441

Mayer, Brown & Platt
Square de Meeus, 19-20 - Bte 4
B-1050 Brussels
Tel : (32) (2) 512-9878
Fax : (32) (2) 511-3305
Steven Brummel, Partner

■ **McGuire, Woods, Battle & Boothe**
US HQ - One James Center
901 East Cary Street
Richmond, VA 23219
Tel : (1) (804) 775-1000
Fax : (1) (804) 775-1061

McGuire, Woods, Battle & Boothe
Avenue Louise, 250 - Bte 64
B-1050 Brussels
Tel : (32) (2) 629-4211
Fax : (32) (2) 629-4222
Donald E. King, Managing Partner
Xavier Van der Mersch, Partner
John W. Barnum, Partner
Jean-Michel FOBE, Associate
Ilse Vandervoort, Associate
Christiane Zuniga, Associate
# of Attorneys specialized in Community Law :
Specialty :   US and EU Regulatory matters - Advice on US and EU Antitrust
                Laws
                Filings with the EC Merger Task Force
                Competition Directorate
                International Trade and Import/Export Control Issues and other
                Regulatory Compliance Matters
                International Corporate Transactions
                Belgian Law Matters
                National and Transnational Tax Matters
                General Corporate Representation

■ **Mc Kenna & Cuneo LLP**
US HQ - 1575 Eye Street NW
Washington, D.C. 20005
Tel : (1) (202) 789-7500
Fax : (1) (202) 789-7756
Contact : A.B. Green

Mc Kenna & Cuneo
Rue des Colonies, 56 - Bte 14
B-1000 Brussels
Tel : (32) (2) 278-1211
Fax : (32) (2) 278-1212
Robert D. Sloan, Managing Partner
Koen Van Maldegem, Partner
Pascal Cardonnel, Partner
# of Attorneys specialised in Community Law : 3
Specialty :   Competition
                 Corporate law
                 Customs
                 Labor Law
                 European Standards
                 Mergers and Acquisitions
                 Environment
                 Tax Law
                 Public Procurement
                 Finance

■ **Morgan, Lewis & Bockius**
US HQ - 20 One Logan Square
Philadelphia, PA 19103 - 6993
Tel : (1) (215) 963-5000
Fax : (1) (215) 963-5299

Morgan, Lewis & Bockius
Rue Guimard, 7
B-1040 Brussels
Tel : (32) (2) 512-5501
Fax : (32) (2) 512-5888
Internet : sina0022@hlb.com
Howard M. Liebman, Managing Partner
Izzet M. Sinan, Partner
S. Alan Hamburger, Partner
Dennis Oswell, Associate
Sara Leventhall, Associate
Julu Gumustekin, Associate
Marcello Hallake, Associate
# of Attorneys specialized in Community Law : 6
Specialty :   Anti-trust / Competition
                Trade
                Customs
                Community Trademarks
                Tax
                Public Procurement
                Environment
                Medical Devices & Pharmaceuticals
                Telecommunications

■ **Morrison & Foerster**
US HQ - 425 Market Street
San Francisco , CA 94105-2482
Tel : (1) (415) 268-7000
Fax : (1) (415) 268-7522

Morrison & Foerster
Avenue Molière, 262
B-1180 Brussels
Tel : (32) (2) 347-0400
Fax : (32) (2) 347-1824
Thomas C. Vinje, Managing Partner
Kathleen Paisley, Lawyer
Penny Turner, Lawyer
# of Attorneys specialized in Community Law : 3
Specialty :   Intellectual Property
              Competition
              Information Technology
              Environment

■ **Oppenheimer, Wolff & Donnelly**
US HQ - 1700 First Bank Bldg
St Paul, MN 55101
Tel : (1) (612) 223-2500
Fax : (1) (612) 224-7504
Contact : M.J. Bleck

Oppenheimer, Wolff & Donnelly
Avenue Louise, 250 - Bte 31
B-1050 Brussels
Tel : (32) (2) 626-0500
Fax : (32) (2) 626-0510
Email : mv03@owd.mhs.compuserve.com
Jean Russotto, Partner in charge
Eric Osterweil, Partner
Frederick.L. Lukoff, Partner
James.H. Searles, Partner
Didier. De Vliegher, Partner
Frank L. Weidema, Partner
Ursula Schliessner, Partner
Philippe R. Logelain, of Counsel
Gretta Goldeman, of Counsel
Amedee Turner, of Counsel
Fiona.M. Carlin, Associate
Erwin De Deyn, Associate
Stefaan De Boeck, Associate
Marie Hélène Jacquemin, Associate

Brian Sheridan, Associate
Erna Moerdijk, Associate
# of Attorneys specialized in Community Law :
Specialty :   Competition :
            Merger, Joint-Companies, R & D
            Executive Concession, Distribution, Patents, Licensing, Know-how, Copyright, Franchising, Trademark, Procedural law
            Commerce : Anti-Dumping, Anti-Subsidies, Protective Measures
            Intracommunity Commerce : Free Circulation of Goods, Services and Capital
            Customs : Origin, Classification, Expertise, Derogation, Reimbursement
            State Subsidies
            Environment / Consumer Protection
            Corporate Law
            Indirect Taxes
            Internal Market
            Product Liability
            Harmonization of Technical standards
            Sectoral Expertise : Banking, Electronics, Chemical Products, Chemical Regulations, Information Technology, Automobiles, Pharmaceuticals, Telecommunications.

■ **Seyfarth, Shaw, Fairweather & Geraldson**
US HQ - 55 Fost Monroe Street
Chicago, IL 60603-5803

Seyfarth, Shaw, Fairweather & Geraldson
Avenue Louise, 500 - Bte 8
B-1050 Brussels
Tel : (32) (2) 647-6025
Website : http://www.seyfarth.com
Email : golub@seyfarth.be
Fax : (32) (2) 640-7071
Martin J. Golub, Partner
# of Attorneys : 2
Specialty :   Business law practice
                Employee Benefits
                Environmental, Safety and Health Law Practice
                Litigation Practice

■ **Sher & Associates, Paul D.**
Avenue Louise, 471
B-1050 Brussels
Tel : (32) (2) 646-5410
Email · 707.6466@mcimail.com
fax : (32) (2) 640-6921
Paul D. Sher, Managing Attorney
Coralie Smets-Gary, Lawyer/Avocat
Marco Dubois, Lawyer/Avocat
Filip Goemans, Avocat/European Counsel
Jef Degrauwe, Avocat/European Counsel

■ **Skadden, Arps, Slate, Meagher & Flom**
US HQ - 919 Third Avenue
New York, NY 10022
Tel : (1) (212) 735-3000
Fax : (1) (212) 735-2000
Contact : **Robert C. Sheehan**

Skadden, Arps, Slate, Meagher & Flom
Avenue Louise, 523 - 3rd Floor
B-1050 Brussels
Tel : (32) (2) 639-0300
Fax : (32) (2) 639-0339
Barry E. Hawk, Resident Partner
Henry L. Huser, Head of EU Merger & Acquisition Practice
Frederic Depoortere, Lawyer
Cynthia Lewis, Lawyer
Nathalie Denaiejer
Nancy Johnson
Ionnis Zervas
Arcanio Cibrario
# of Attorneys specialized in Community Law : 13
Specialty :   **Barry E. Hawk** : Competition, Public Procurement, State
Subsidies, Telecommunications, Energy, Transportation
Henry L. Huser : Competition, Control of Mergers
Nathalie Denaiejer : Competition, State Subsidies, Public
Procurement, Telecommunications
Nancy Johnson : Competition, Control of Mergers
Ionnis Zervas : Competition, State Subsidies, Public
Procurement
Arcanio Cibrario : Competition, State Subsidies, Environment
Cynthia Lewis : Competition, Control of Mergers
Frederic Depoortere : Competition, Control of Mergers,
Environment

■ **Squire, Sanders & Dempsey**
US HQ - 4900 Key Tower
127 Public Square
Cleveland, OHIO 44114 - 1304
Tel : (1) (216) 479-8500
Fax : (1) (216) 479-8780

Squire, Sanders & Dempsey
Avenue Louise, 165 - Bte 15
B-1050 Brussels
Tel : (32) (2) 627-1111
Fax : (32) (2)627-1100
Brian Harnett, Partner
Marco Hickey, Associate
Heidi Pemberton, Associate
Guy J. Pevtchin, Senior EU Law Counsel
Marie-Thérèse Rainey, Associate
Thomas J. Ramsey, Partner
Stephane Rating, Associate
# of Attorneys specialized in Community Law :
Specialty :   All Areas of European Community Law and in particular :
                    - Anti-Trust
                    - Dumping
                    - Mergers

■ **Stewart & Stewart**
US HQ - 2100 M Street NW
Suite 200
Washington DC 20037
Tel : (1) (202) 785-4185
Fax : (1) (202) 466-1286/87/88

Stewart and Stewart
Boulevard Dewandre, 13
B-6000 Charleroi
Tel : (32) (71) 325131
Fax : (32) (71) 323526
Email : 100771.1253
Bernard. Spinoit, Counsel
Anne Wese, Counsel
# of Attorneys specialized in Community Law : 2
Specialty :   **Bernard Spinoit** : Antidumping, Customs, Competition
                    Anne Wese : Antidumping, Customs, Competition

■ Thompson, Hine & Flory LLP

US HQ - 3900 Society Center
124 Public Square
Cleveland, Ohio 45202
Tel : (1) (216) 566-5500
Fax : (1) (216) 566-5800

Thompson, Hine & Flory PLL
Avenue Louise, 123
B-1050 Brussels
Tel : (32) (2) 543-7860
Fax : (32) (2)543-7866
Ludo M. Deklerck, Lawyer
# of Attorneys specialized in Community Law : 2
Specialty :   Business Organizational Matters
Commercial Transactions
Dispute Resolution
Distribution and Marketing
Financing
Franchising
Immigration
International Trade Regulation
International Transactions
Joint Ventures
Labor and Employment
Mergers and Acquisitions
Real Estate and Site Selection
Taxation
Technology Transfers
Trademark
Unfair Competition
Venture Planning
EU Developments
Doing Business in Belgium

■ **Weil, Gotshal & Manges LLP**
US HQ - 767 Fifth Avenue
New York, NY 10153
Tel : (1) (212) 310-8000
Fax : (1) (212) 310-8007
Email : alan.levine@weil.com
Contact : **A. Levine**

Weil, Gotshal & Manges LLP
Avenue Louise, 81 - Bte 9-10
B-1050 Brussels
Tel : (32) (2) 543-7460
Fax : (32) (2) 543-7489
Email : randolph.tritell@weil.com
Randolph W. Tritell, Resident Partner
David Cantor, Resident Partner
George Metaxas-Maranghidis, Lawyer
David Chijner, Lawyer
Stanislas De Peuter, Lawyer
# of Attorneys specialized in Community Law : 5
Specialty :   **Randolph W. Tritell** : Competition, Telecommunications, Commerce
David Cantor : Telecommunicatioons, Public Procurement
George Metaxas-Maranghidis : Intellectual Property, Competition, Telecommunications, Commerce, Public Procurement
David Chijner : Competition, Corporate Law
Stanislas De Peuter : Competition

■ **White & Case**
US HQ - 1158 Avenue of the Americas
New York, NY 10036-2787
Tel : (1) (212) 819-8200
Fax : (1) (212) 354-8113

White & Case
Avenue Louise, 306-310
B-1050 Brussels
Tel : (32) (2) 647-0589
Fax : (32) (2) 647-1675

Werner Vanderhaege, Counsel
Pontus Lindfelt, Associate
Margaret Wachenfeld, Associate
Werner Van Lembergen, Associate
Anna Garcia Bello, Associate
# of Attorneys specialized in Community Law : 4
Specialty :   **Pontus Lindfelt** : Competition; Antidumping, Mergers & Acquisitions
Margaret Wachenfeld : Environment, Commerce / Customs
Werner Vanderhaeghe : Competition, Environment, Merger & Acquisitions
Werner Van Lembergen : Competition

■ **Wilmer, Cutler & Pickering**
US HQ - 2445 M Street NW
Washington DC 20037 - 1420
Tel : (1) (202) 663-6000
Fax : (1) (202) 663-6363
Contact : **W.T. Lake**

Wilmer, Cutler & Pickering
Rue de la Loi ,15
B-1040 Brussels
Tel : (32) (2) 285-4900
Fax : (32) (2) 285-4949
James.S. Venit, Partner
Marc. Hansen, Partner
Andreas Weitbrecht, Partner
Paul A. von Hehn, Partner
# of Attorneys specialized in Community Law : 13
Specialty :   Community Regulations in the following areas :
                        - Telecommunications, Medias
                        - Intellectual Property
                        - Competition
                        - Commercial Law in the EU
                        - Representation of Clients in European transactions

■ **Winthrop, Stimson, Putnam & Roberts**
US HQ - One Battery Park Plaza
Tel : (1) (212) 858-1000
Fax : (1) (212) 858-1500

Winthrop, Stimson, Putnam & Roberts
Rue du Taciturne, 42
B-1000 Brussels
Tel : (32) (2) 230-1392
Fax: (32) (2) 230-9288
Raymond S. Calamaro, Lawyer
Maria Patricia Azevedo, Partner in Charge
Rita Rique Pearson, Lawyer
# of Attorneys specialized in Community Law : 3
Specialty :   Mary Patricia Azevedo
                        Rita Rique Pearson
                        Community Policy and Regulation
                        Financial Services

SUMMARY
AMERICAN LAW FIRMS IN BELGIUM

Akin, Gump, Strauss, Hauer & Feld
Avenue Louise, 65 - Bte 7
B-1050 Brussels
Tel : (32) (2) 535-2911
Fax : (32) (2) 535-2900

Allen & Overy
Rue de la Loi, 99 - Bte 8
B-1040 Brussels
Tel : (32) (2) 230-2791
Fax : (32) (2) 230-6613

Baker and Mc Kenzie
Boulevard du Régent, 40
B-1000 Brussels
Tel : (32) (2) 506-3611
Fax : (32) (2) 511-6280

Broderick Terry R
Avenue Louise, 475 - Bte 8
B-1050 Brussels
Tel : (32) (2) 649-0019
Fax : (32) (2) 646-0152

Cleary, Gottlieb, Steen & Hamilton
Rue de la Loi, 23 - Bte 5
B-1040 Brussels
Tel : (32) (2) 287-2000
Fax : (32) (2) 231-1661 & 230-1635

Coudert Brothers
Avenue Louise, 149 - Bte 8
B-1050 Brussels
Tel : (32) (2) 542-1811
Fax : (32) (2) 539-2888 & 537-2710

Covington & Burling
Avenue des Arts, 44 - Bte 8
B-1040 Brussels
Tel : (32) (2) 549-5230
Fax : (32) (2) 502-1598

Dechert, Price & Rhoads
Avenue Louise, 65 - Bte 4
B-1050 Brussels
Tel : (32) (2) 535-5411
Fax : (32) (2) 535-5400

Dobson & Pinci
Avenue Franklin Roosevelt, 4
B-1050 Brussels
Tel : (32)(2) 647-0700
Fax : (32) (2) 647-6440

Dorsey & Whitney
Square de Meeûs, 35
B-1040 Brussels
Tel : (32) (2) 504-4611
Fax : (32) (2) 504-4646

Foley & Lardner
Avenue Louise, 283 - Bte 5
B-1050 Brussels
Tel : (32) (2) 646-2777
Fax : (32) (2) 646-7574

Hogan & Hartson
Avenue des Arts, 41
B-1040 Brussels
Tel : (32) (2) 505-0911
Fax : (32) (2) 502-2860

Hunton & Williams
Avenue Louise, 106
B-1050 Brussels
Tel : (32) (2) 646-0010
Fax : (32) (2) 646-0246

Jones, Day, Repvis & Pogue
Avenue Louise, 480 - 7th Floor
ITT Tower
B-1050 Brussels
Tel : (32) (2) 645-1411
Fax : (32) (2) 645-1445

Keller & Heckman
Boulevard Louis Schmidt, 87
B-1040 Brussels
Tel : (32) (2) 732-5280
Fax : (32) (2) 732-5392

Kelley, Drye & Warren
Avenue Louise, 106 - Bte 7
B-1050 Brussels
Tel : (32) (2) 646 1110
Fax : (32) (2) 640-0589

Kilpatrick Stockton
Avenue Louise, 149 - Bte 15
B-1050 Brussels
Tel : (32) (2) 533-0300
Fax : (32) (2) 534-8638

Le Boeuf, Lamb, Green & Macrae
Avenue des Arts, 19 H
B-1000 Brussels
Tel : (32) (2) 227-0900
Fax : (32) (2) 227-0909

Mayer, Brown & Platt
Square de Meeûs, 19-20
B-1040 Brussels
Tel : (32) (2) 512-9878
Fax : (32) (2) 511-3305

Mc Guire, Woods, Battle & Boothe
Avenue Louise, 250 - Bte 64
B-1050 Brussels
Tel : (32) (2) 629-4211
Fax : (32) (2) 629-4222

Mc Kenna & Cuneo
Rue des Colonies, 56 - Bte 14
B-1000 Brussels
Tel : (32) (2) 278-1211
Fax : (32) (2) 278-1212

Morgan, Lewis & Bockius
Rue Guimard, 7
B-1040 Brussels
Tel : (32) (2) 512-5501
Fax : (32) (2) 512-5888

Morrison & Foerster
Avenue Molière, 262
B-1180 Brussels
Tel : (32) (2) 347-0400
Fax : (32) (2) 347-1824

Oppenheimer, Wolff & Donelly
Avenue Louise, 250 - Bte 31
B-1050 Brussels
Tel : (32) (2) 626-0500
Fax : (32) (2) 626-0510

Seyfarth, Shaw, Fairweather & Geraldson
Avenue Louise, 500 - Bte 8
B-1050 Brussels
Tel : (32) (2) 647-6025
Fax : (32) (2) 640-7071

Sher & Associates, Paul D.
Avenue Louise, 471
B-1050 Brussels
Tel : (32) (2) 646-5410
Fax : (32) (2) 640-6921

Skadden, Arps, Slate, Meagher & Flom
Avenue Louise, 523 - 3rd Floor
B-1050 Brussels
Tel : (32) (2) 639-0300
Fax : (32) (2) 639-0339

Squire, Sanders & Dempsey
Avenue Louise, 165 - Bte 15
B-1050 Brussels
Tel : (32) (2) 627-1111
Fax : (32) (2) 627-1100

Stewart & Stewart
Boulevard Dewandre, 13
B-6000 Charleroi
Tel : (32) (71) 32 51 31
Fax: (32) (71) 32 35 26

Thompson, Hine & Flory PLL
Avenue Louise, 123
B-1050 Brussels
Tel : (32) (2) 543-7860
Fax : (32) (2) 543-7866

Weil, Gotshal & Manges LLP
Avenue Louise, 81 - Bte 9-10
B-1050 Brussels
Tel : (32) (2) 543-7460
Fax : (32) (2) 543-7489

White & Case
Avenue Louise, 306-310
B-1050 Brussels
Tel : (32) (2) 647-0589
Fax : (32) (2) 647-1675

Wilme, Cutler & Pickering
Rue de la Loi, 15
B-1040 Brussels
Tel : (32) (2) 285-4900
Fax : (32) (2) 285-4949

Winthrop, Stimson, Putnam & Roberts
Rue du Taciturne, 42
B-1000 Brussels
Tel : (32) (2) 230-1392
Fax : (32) (2) 230-9288

REPRESENTATIVE ACTIVITIES OF AMERICAN LAW FIRMS BASED IN BRUSSELS

Corporate Practice :

- Providing new businesses with practical advice on choice of entity, capital structure, financing and site selection issues.
- Negotiating distributor, franchise, sales agency and complex agreements in various EU member states on behalf of a range of multinational corporations to individual entrepreneurs.
- Assisting individuals, existing businesses and venture capitalists in planning for and implementing acquisitions, mergers sales and restructuring.
- Organizing joint-ventures and cross-border investments
- Providing general corporate counsel to numerous businesses with which the firms have developed long standing relationships

Environmental, Health and Safety and Product Standards Practice

- Assisting multinational companies in organizing European and worldwide corporate environmental management and audit programs.
- Organizing and supervising environmental due diligence investigations and advising on potential liability for contamination and personal injury in acquisitions or other business contexts.
- Advising multinational companies on environmental permitting and plant construction and operating requirements in EU member states and other European countries (i.e. Eastern Europe).
- Advising chemical, electronics , consumer goods, and other companies concerning EU and national health and safety regulations.
- Advising chemical, petrochemical, and oil companies concerning soil remediation, cleanup orders, and related negotiations with governmental agencies and private parties.
- Advising chemical, consumer goods, food, and electronics companies on EU and national packaging, labeling, marketing and related reporting obligations.

- Assisting trade associations concerning the range of EU and national environmental measures, including, in particular, measures with the potential to cause trade barriers (e.g. electronic take-back measures, eco-labels, and substance restrictions).
- Analyzing and drafting position papers on EU and national legislative proposals concerning eco-taxes, packaging and product take-back, eco-auditing systems; waste shipment, landfills and liability; and
- Assisting companies i.e. electronics, vehicle, etc., on EU product stand-ardization and certification (e.g. EU markings).

Chemicals, Pharmaceuticals, Food and Drug and Biotech Practice

- Advising pharmaceuticals, medical devices and biotechnology companies on (pre) clinical trials and studies, registration and licensing, reimbursement, labeling, instructions for use, post-marketing, surveillance, marketing and advertising and related matters.
- Assisting chemical companies in connection with chemical notifications, labeling and marketing of dangerous substances and dangerous preparations, and
- Advising additives, food contact and food packaging companies on regulatory issues, including novel foods and liability issues.

Telecommunications practice

- Advising clients on a range of competition issues for the EU telecommunications market

Labour Practice

- Counseling employers of all sizes on a wide range of labor matters including drafting employment and non-competition agreements and structuring compensation arrangements.
- Counselling clients on potential problems associated with Belgium immigration laws.
- Assisting with issues related to business income, salary splits, taxation of foreign executives, avoidance of double taxation, and the fiscal regime applicable to nonresidents in Belgium.

- Advising clients on social security issues, welfare benefits, social security for expatriates and nonresidents and the like.
- Representing clients in collective labor issues, such as collective layoffs, closings, downsizings, transfers of undertakings, and negotiations of collective labor agreements.
- Representing clients regarding hiring policies, working conditions, secondment from Belgium or Europe, termination severance packages.

International Trade Regulation Practice

- Consulting on international trade regulations issues, including export licensing, unfair import pratices, anti-boycott practices, foreign corrupt pratices, litigation and legislation.

Technology Transfers Practice

- Negotiating patent licenses and technology transfer agreements and securing clients' rights to worldwide intellectual property protection.

Distribution Marketing Practice

- Negotiating incentive packages and investment grants with the Belgian Federal and Regional Governments and searching " Coordination Center " and " Distribution Center " status for companies with centralized European operations in Belgium.

Litigation Practice

- Representing private parties challenging governmental decisions before the Belgian Administrative Supreme Court.
- Representing private clients before Belgian Courts in cases ranging from commercial litigation to bankruptcy procedures.
- Representing companies in unfair trade pratices litigation.
- Representing multinational and local companies in labor matters, such as breach of contracts and termination issues before Belgian Courts.

ALPHABETICAL LISTING OF ATTORNEYS

ADKINS Bernardine, Associate, Dechert, Price & Rhoads
ANDREWS Philippe, Lawyer, Keller & Heckman
ART Jean-Yves, Partner, Coudert Brothers
AZEVEDO, Maria Patricia, Partner in charge, Winthrop, Stimson, Putnam & Roberts
BARAGONA Katarine C., Resident Associate
BARNUM John W., Partner, McGuire, Woods, Battle & Boothe
BERGKAMP Lucas Prof., Resident Counsel, Hunton & Williams
BERRA Jean-Louis, Resident Associate, Hunton& Williams
BLANCHARD Charles A., Managing Partner, Hunton & Williams
BOURGEOIS Hendrick, Lawyer, Jones, Day, Reavis & Pogue
BOURGEOIS, Partner, Akin,Gump,Strauss,Hauer & Feld
BRODERICK Terry R., Independent Lawyer
BRUMMEL Steven, Partner, Mayer, Brown & Platt
BUHART Jacques, Partner, Coudert Brothers
BURKA Robert A., Foley & Lardner (Washington DC)
BUSTIN George, Partner, Cleary, Gottlieb, Steen & Hamilton
BUYTAERT Thierry, Lawyer, Jones, Day, Reavis & Pogue
CALAMARO Raymond S., Lawyer, Winthrop , Stimson, Putnam & Roberts
CAMBRE Nicole, Resident Associate
CANTOR David, Resident Partner, Weil, Gotshal & Manges
CARDONNEL Pascal, Partner, Mc Kenna & Cuneo
CARLIN Fiona M., Associate, Oppenheimer, Wolff & Donnelly
CHIJNER David, Lawyer, Weil, Gotshal & Manges
CIBRARIO Arcanio, Lawyer, Skadden, Arps, Meagher & Flom
COGELS Hervé, Partner, Coudert Brothers
DE BOECK Stefaan, Associate, Oppenheimer, Wolff & Donnelly
DE DEYN Erwin, Associate, Oppenheimer, Wolff & Donnelly
DE HEMPTINNE Patrice, Resident Associate, Hunton & Williams
DE PEUTER Stanislas, Lawyer, Weil, Gotshal & Manges
DE VLIEGHER Didier, Partner, Oppenheimer, Wolff & Donnelly
DEGRAUWE Jef, European Counsel, Sher & Associates
DEJONGE Alain, Akin , Gump, Strauss, Hauer & Feld
DEKLERK Ludo M., Lawyer, Thompson, Hine & Flory
DELLA ROSA, Lawyer, Akin,Gump, Strauss, Hauer & Feld
DENAIEJER Nathalie, Lawyer, Skadden, Arps, Meagher & Flom
DEPOORTERE Frederic, Lawyer, Skadden, Arps, Meagher & Flom
DEWITTE Martine, Partner,Akin,Gump,Strauss,Hauer & Feld

DOBSON David M., Lawyer, Dobson & Pinci
DOLMANS Maurits, Partner, Cleary, Gottlieb, Steen & Hamilton
DUBOIS Marco, Lawyer, Sher & Associates
ELEY Claude v.S., Partner in charge, Hogan & Hartson
EWERT Daniel Dr., Foley & Lardner (Brussels)
FOBE Jean-Michel, Associate, McGuire, Woods, Battle & Boothe
FOGT Howard W., Foley & Lardner (Washington DC)
GABRIEL François, Lawyer, Baker & Mc Kenzie
GARCIA BELLO Ana, Associate, White & Case
GERADIN Damien, Lawyer, Coudert Brothers
GERRITS, Lawyer, Akin, Gump, Strauss, Hauer & Feld
GHYSBRECHT Jacques, Partner, Baker & Mc Kenzie
GILSON Nathalie, Lawyer, Coudert Brothers
GLAZER Barry D. , Partner, Dorsey & Whitney
GOEMANS Filip, European Counsel, Sher & Associates
GOLDEMAN Gretta, of Counsel, Oppenheimer, Wolff & Donnelly
GOLUB Martin J., Partner, Seyfarth, Shaw, Fairweather & Geraldson
GRAF Bernd U , Partner, Dorsey & Whitney
GROLIG Otto, Partner, Baker & Mc Kenzie
GHUMUSTEKIN Julu, Associate, Morgan, Lewis & Bockius
HALLAKE Marcello, Associate, Morgan, Lewis & Bockius
HAMBURGER S.Alan , Partner Morgan, Lewis & Bockius
HANSEN Marc, Partner, Wilmer, Cutler & Pickering
HARFST David L., Lawyer, Covington & Burling
HARNETT Brian, Partner, Squire, Sanders & Dempsey
HARRISON David M. Senior Assistant, Allen & Overy
HAWK Barry E., Resident Partner, Skadden, Arps, Slate, Meagher & Flom
HAWKES Leonard W.N., Partner, Le Bouf, Lamb, Green & Macrae
HELLER Frederick K. Jr., Managing Partner, Kilpatrick Stockton
HENDRICKS Frederic, Resident Associate, Hunton & Williams
HERTEN Paul, Lawyer, Baker & Mc Kenzie
HICKEY Marco, Associate, Squire, Sanders & Dempsey
HINNEKENS Luc, Partner, Baker & Mc Kenzie
HOUBEN Luc G., Partner, Jones, Day, Reavis & Pogue
HUNTER Roszell, Resident Partner, Hunton & Williams
HUSER Henry L., Head of EU M.& A Practice, Skadden, Arps, Meagher
    & Flom
HUYGHE Alain, Lawyer, Baker & Mc Kenzie
JACQUEMIN Marie Helene, Associate, Oppenheimer, Wolff & Donnelly
JOHNSON Nancy, Lawyer, Skadden, Arps, Meagher & Flom
JORIS Jean-Louis, Partner, Cleary, Gottlieb, Steen & Hamilton

JOSEPH Ghislain T., Partner, Jones, Day, Reavis & Pogue
KARLSON Kent S., Lawyer, Coudert Brothers
KING Donald E., Managing Partner, McGuire, Woods, Battle & Boothe
KNABLE Ilene, Foley & Lardner (Washington DC)
KNAPP Wolfgang, Partner, Cleary, Gottlieb, Steen & Hamilton
KOCH Norbert, Partner, Jones, Day, Reavis & Pogue
LAMAL Guido, Lawyer, Hogan & Hartson
LANGLOIS Jacques, Managing Partner, Akin,Gump,Strauss,Hauer & Feld
LECHIEN Dominique, Lawyer, Baker & Mc Kenzie
LEHMANN Etienne, Resident Associate, Hunton & Williams
LEVENTHALL Sara, Associate, Morgan, Lewis & Bockius
LEVITT Melinda F. Foley & Lardner (Washington DC)
LEWIS Cynthia, Lawyer, Skadden, Arps, Slate, Meagher & Flom
LIEBMAN Howard M. , Managing Partner, Morgan, Lewis & Bockius
LINDFELT Pontus P., Associate, White & Case
LOCKETT James K., Partner, Le Bouf, Lamb, Green & Macrae
LOGELAIN Philippe R., of Counsel, Oppenheimer, Wolff & Donnelly
LOGIE André, Associate, Hogan & Hartson
LONTINGS Dirk, Lawyer, Hogan & Hartson
LUFF David, Lawyer, Coudert Brothers
LUKOFF Frederick L., Partner, Oppenheimer, Wolff & Donnelly
MAES Ignace, Partner, Baker & Mc Kenzie
MAGREMANNE Jean-Pierre, Associate, Dechert, Price and Rhoads
MANSFIELD Philip, Assistant, Allen & Overy
MARANTIS Dimitrios, Lawyer, Akin, Gump, Strauss, Hauer & Feld
MENCIK VON ZEBINSKY Alexandre, Lawyer, Keller & Heckman
METAXAS-MARANGHIDIS George, Lawyer, Weil, Gotshal & Manges
MEYERS Jan, Partner, Cleary, Gottlieb, Steen & Hamilton
MODRALL Jay, Partner, Cleary, Gottlieb, Steen & Hamilton
MOERDIJK Erna, Associate, Oppenheimer, Wolff & Donnelly
MONTFORT Jean-Philippe, Lawyer, Keller & Heckman
MUELLER-IBOLD Till, Special Councel, Cleary, Gottlieb, Steen & Hamilton
MUYLLE Koen, Resident Associate, Hunton & Williams
OBERREIT Walter, Partner, Cleary, Gottlieb, Steen & Hamilton
OBERST Gerald; Lawyer, Hogan & Hartson
OREMAN Filip, Partner, Cleary, Gottlieb, Steen & Hamilton
OSTERWEIL Eric, Partner, Oppenheimer, Wolff & Donnelly
OSWELL Dennis, Associate, Morgan, Lewis & Bockius
OVERBURY Colin, Consultant, Allen & Overy
PAISLEY Kathleen, Lawyer, Morrison & Foerster
PEMBERTON Heidi, Associate, Squire, Sanders & Dempsey

PEVTCHIN Guy J., Senior EU Law Counsel, Squire, Sanders & Dempsey
RAHMAN Pascale F., Counsel, Kilpatrick Stockton
RAINEY Marie-Thérèse, Associate, Squire, Sanders & Dempsey
RAITING Stephane, Associate, Squire, Sanders & Dempsey
RAMSEY Thomas J., Partner, Squire, Sanders & Dempsey
REDING Jacques, Partner, Cleary, Gottlieb, Steen & Hamilton
REYNOLDS Michael J., Resident Partner, Allen & Overy
RIQUE PEARSON Rita, Lawyer, Winthrop, Stimson, Putnam & Roberts
RUSSOTTO Jean, Partner in charge, Oppenheimer, Wolff & Donnelly
SAN BENTO DE MENEZES José, Lawyer, Coudert Brothers
SAVIGNY Jean, Resident Partner, Keller & Heckman
SCASSELLATI Giuseppe, Partner, Cleary, Gottlieb, Steen & Hamilton
SCHLIESSNER Ursula, Partner, Oppenheimer, Wolff & Donnelly
SCHOLLEN Anne, Associate, Dechert, Price and Rhoads
SCULIER Pierre, Lawyer, Baker & Mc Kenzie
SCHAERZ Melvin A., Partner, Decher, Price & Rhoads
SEARLES James H., Partner, Oppenheimer, Wolff & Donnelly
SHER Paul D., Managing Attorney, Sher & Associates
SHERIDAN Brian, Associate, Oppenheimer, Wolff & Donnelly
SINAN Izzet M., of Counsel, Morgan, Lewis & Bockius
SIRAGUSA Mario, Partner, Cleary, Gottlieb, Steen & Hamilton
SISTILLI Anthony, Lawyer, Dobson & Pinci
SLOAN Robert D., Managing Partner, Mc Kenna & Cuneo
SLOOTSMAN Jozef, Lawyer, Baker & Mc Kenzie
SMETS-GARY Coralie, Lawyer, Sher & Associates
SOUSSAN Guy, Partner, Le Bouf, Lamb, Green & Macrae
SPINKS Stephen O., Partner, Coudert Brothers
SPINOIT Bernard, Counsel, Stewart & Stewart
SUBIOTTO Roman, Partner, Cleary, Gottlieb, Steen & Hamilton
TEMKO Richard J., Resident Attorney, Dechert, Price & Rhoads
TIELEMANS Henriette, Lawyer, Covington & Burling
TRITELL Randolph W., Resident Partner, Weil, Gotshal & Manges
TURNER Amédée, of Counsel, Oppenheimer, Wolff & Donnelly
TURNER Penny, Lawyer, Morrison & Foerster
TUYTSCHAEVER Filip, Associate, Hogan & Hartson
VAN BESEN Jan, Lawyer, Akin, Gump, Strauss, Hauer & Feld
VAN DER MERSCH Xavier, Partner, McGuire, Woods, Battle & Boothe
VAN LANDUYT André, Lawyer, Keller & Heckman
VAN LEMBERGEN Werner, Associate, White & Case
VAN LIEDERKERKE Dirk, Lawyer, Coudert Brothers
VAN MALDEGEM, Partner, Mc Kenna & Cuneo

VAN MELLAERT George, Associate, Dechert, Price & Rhoads
VANDER SCHUEREN Paulette, Partner, Coudert Brothers
VANDERHAEGE Werner, Counsel, White & Case
VANDERVOORT Ilse, Associate, Mc Guire, Woods, Battle & Boothe
VANHAERENTS Koen, Lawyer, Baker & Mc Kenzie
VENIT James S., Partner, Wilmer, Cutler & Pickering
VERHAEGE Peter, Partner, Akin,Gump,Strauss,Hauer & Feld
VIG Vernon, Partner, Le Bouf, Lamb, Green & Macrae
VINJE Thomas C., Managing Partner, Morrison & Foerster
VON HEHN Paul A., Partner, Wilmer, Cutler & Pickering
WACHENFELD Margaret, Associate, White & Case
WEIDEMA Frank L., Partner, Oppenheimer, Wolff & Donnelly
WEITBRECHT Andreas, Partner, Wilmer, Cutler & Pickering
WINCKLER Antoine, Partner, Cleary, Gottlieb, Steen & Hamilton
YERXA Rufus, Partner, Akin,Gump,Strauss,Hauer & Feld
ZANNONI Lisa, Associate, Hogan & Hartson
ZERVAS Ionnis, Lawyer, Skadden, Arps, Meagher & Flom
ZUNIGA Christiane, Associate, Mc Guire, Woods, Battle & Boothe

CHAPTER 12
US BANKS REPRESENTED IN BRUSSELS

■ **Bank of America NT & SA**
Uitbreidingstraat, 180 - Box 6
B-2600 Antwerp
Tel: (32) (2) 280-4211
Fax: (32) (2) 239-6109
William Nijboer, Vice-President, Regional Manager Benelux
Richard Challinor, Vice-President, Manager-GPS European Regional Center
Commercial Banking

Other Facilities:
Avenue Van Niewenhuyse 6
B-1160 Brussels
Tel: (32) (2) 663-2100

Branch of :   Bank of America NT & SA
                555 California Street
                San Francisco, CA 94137

■ **Bank of New York, The**
Avenue des Arts, 35
B-1040 Brussels
Tel: (32) (2) 545-8111
E-mail: mbuyst@email.bony.com
Fax: (32) (2) 545-8000
Paul Bodart, Senior Vice-President
Marc Buyst, Vice-President
Keith Whitelock, Vice -President

■ **Chase Manhattan Bank,The**
Avenue Louise, 326 - Boîte 51
B-1050 Brussels
Tel: (32) (2) 629-5811
Fax: (32) (2) 629-5837
Benoit Struyle de Swienlande, Vice-President and General Manager
F. Verlinden, Vice-President
N. Boullart, Vice-President Banking

Branch of :   Chase Manhattan Bank (The)
                  270 Park Avenue
                  New York, NY 10017-2036

■ **Citibank N.A.**
Boulevard Général Jacques, 263g
B-1050 Brussels
Tel: (32) (2) 626-5111
Website: http://www.cit.bank.com
Fax: (32) (2) 626-5584
Michael M; Roberts, Managing Director Citibank NA
Victor Toledo, Country Corporate Officer, Managing Director Citibank SA
Armand d'Aspremont, Head European Corporate Group
Olaf Neubert, General Manager Citibank Cards Division
Pierre Hautain, General Manager, Diners Club Benelux
Commercial Banking/ Investment Banking/Consumer Banking/Credit Cards

Branch of: Citibank NA
                 399 Park Avenue
                 New York, NY 10043

■ Euroclear Operations Centre
Boulevard Emile Jacqmain, 151
B-1210 Brussels
Tel: (32) (2) 224-1211
Fax: (32) (2) 224-1287
Luc Bomans, Managing Director & General Manager
Ignace R. Combes, Managing Director & Head Market Services Division
Martine Dinne, Managing Director & Head Commercial Division
Richard C. Evans, Managing Director & Head of Domestic Securities Division
Pierre Francotte, Managing Director, Resident Counsel & Head of Legal Division
Theo Van Engelard, Vice-President Controller & Head of Financial Division

Subsidiary of: Morgan Guaranty Trust Co of New York
        60 Wall Street
        NewYork, NY 10260-0060

■ Fifth Third Bank
European Representation Office
Avenue de Tervuren, 311 - Suite 9
B-1150 Brussels
Tel: (32) (2) 779-3145
E-mail: 103504.3243@compuserve.com
Fax: (32) (2) 779-3146
John K. Perez, Chief Representative, Assistant Vice-President
Maintaining, developing contacts with European parent corporations, correspondent banks, American companies selling abroad and companies looking to invest in Ohio, Kentucky and Indiana.

Representative Office of: Fifth Third Bank
        38 Fountain Square Plaza
        Cincinnati, Ohio

■ JP Morgan
Avenue des Arts, 35
B-1040 Brussels
Tel: (32) (2) 508-8211
Fax: (32) (2) 508-8334
Christian Jacobs, Managing Director and Senior Banker
Herv, Huas, Managing Director and Chairman of the Management Committee
Theo Van Engeland, Chief Operating Officer

Branch of: Morgan Guaranty Trust Co of New York
60 Wall Street
New York, NY 10015

CHAPTER 13
US ACCOUNTING FIRMS

■ **Arthur Andersen & Co**
69 West Washington Street
Chicago, IL 60602

Arthur Andersen & Co
Avenue des Arts, 56
B-1040 Brussels
Tel : (32) (2) 510-4211
Fax : (32) (2) 513-0862

Marcel Asselberghs & Co
(Office of Arthur Andersen & Co)
B-1040 Brussels
Tel : (32) (2) 510-4499
Fax : (32) (2) 513-0862

■ **Price Waterhouse**
1251 Avenue of the Americas
New York, NY 10020

Price Waterhouse s.c.
Woluwedal 30
B-1932 Zaventem
Tel : (32) (2) 713-7000
Fax : (32) (2) 725-6955

Pauwels & Partners
(Member Firm of Price Waterhouse)
Woluwedal 30
B-1932 Zaventem
Tel : (32) (2) 713-7000
Fax : (32) (2) 725-6955

Office: De Keyserlei 5, Box 11A
          B-2018 Antwerp
          Tel : (32) (3) 233-3640

■ Ernst & Young International
787 Seventh Avenue
New York, NY 10019

Ernst & Young
Avenue Marcel Thiry, 204
B-1200 Brussels
Tel : (32) (2) 774-9111
Fax : (32) (2) 774-9090

■ KPMG
345 Park Avenue
New York, NY 10154

KPMG Marcel Bellen & Co
(Associated Firm of KPMG)
Rue Neerveld, 101-103
B-1200 Brussels
Tel : (32) (2) 773-3611
Fax : (32) (2) 772-3305

Office: St.Petersvliet 7 - Box 3
          B-1200 Antwerp
          Tel : (32) (3) 231-6763

■ Ernst & Whinney International
787 Seventh Avenue
New York, NY 10019

Bertel, Swolfs, Van Cutsen & Co
(Member Firm of Ernst & Whinney International)
Avenue Louise, 523 - Boîte 31
B-1050 Brussels
Tel: (32) (2) 640-2920
Fax: (32) (2) 641-9095

■ **Coopers & Lybrand**
1251 Avenue of the Americas
New York, NY 10020

Coopers & Lybrand
Avenue de Tervuren, 270-272
B-1150 Brussels
Tel: (32) (2) 771-2150
Fax: (32) (2) 771-2399

Office: De Keyserlei 58 - Box 46
           B-1200 Antwerp

Jacobs, Eeckhout & Co
(Associated Firm of Coopers & Lybrand)
Avenue de Tervuren 270-272 - Box 27
B-1150 Brussels
Tel: (32) (2) 771-2150
Fax: (32) (2) 771-2399

CHAPTER 14
US MEDIA AND NEWSPAPERS
REPRESENTED IN BRUSSELS

AP-Dow Jones
IPC - boulevard Charlemagne, 1 - Bte 49
B - 1041 Brussels
Tel : (32) (2) 285-0131
Tel : (32) (2) 285-0130
Fax : (32) (2) 285-0156
Fax : (32) (2) 285-0134
E-mail: pgoldstein@am.trees.ap.org
Carthy Grainne
Peter Goldstein (Bureau Chief)

AP-Dow Jones
IPC boulevard Charlemagne, 1
B - 1041 Brussels
Tel : (32) (2) 285-0132
Tel : (32) (2) 285-0130
Fax : (32) (2) 285-0156
Jonathan Stearns
David W. Tweed

Associated Press
IPC boulevard Charlemagne, 1 - Bte 49
B - 1041 Brussels
Tel : (32) (2) 285-0112
Tel : (32) (2) 285-0111
Tel : (32) (2) 285-0113
Tel : (32) (2) 285-0114
Tel : (32) (2) 285-0140
Tel : (32) (2) 285-0121
Fax : (32) (2) 285-0155
Fax : (32) (2) 285-0156
Paul David Ames
Raf Casert
Claude Colart

Stephanie Griffith
Koenrad Santersman
Jeffrey Ulbrich
Robert J. Wielaard (Bureau Chief)

Associated Press (German Service)
Bd Charlemagne, 1 - Bte 49
B - 1040 Brussels
Tel : (32) (2) 285-0115
Fax : (32) (2) 285-0155
Claudia Kemmer

Bloomberg Business News
IPC - Bd Charlemagne, 1
B - 1041 Brussels
Tel : (32) (2) 280-0126
Fax : (32) (2) 230-2514
Caroline Jacobs (32) (2) 285-4300
Raphael Minder

Bloomberg News
IPC bd Charlemagne, 1 - Bte 28
B - 1041 Brussels
Tel : (32) (2) 280-0126
Fax : (32) (2) 230-2514
James Neuger (Bureau Chief)
Robert Mc Leod (32) (2) 285-4303

Bridge News
IPC-Boulevard Charlemagne, 1 - Boite 14
B-1041 Brussels
Tel : (32) (2) 231-1450
Fax : (32)(2) 230-0518
David Thomas
Marleen Van Parys

Bureau of National Affairs
Rue des Platanes, 39
B - 1040 Brussels
Tel : (32) (2) 732-3740
James Joseph Kirwin

Business International
Av. Georges Henri, 27
B - 1200 Brussels
Tel : (32) (2) 223-0495
Fax : (32) (2) 271-4102
Elizabeth De Bony

Business Week
Avenue de la Floride, 118
B - 1180 Brussels
Tel : (32) (2) 375-7016
Fax : (32) (2) 374-3426
William Echikson Tel : (32) (2) 374-2310
Linda Bernier

CNN (Cable News Network)
Chaussee de Louvain, 515
B - 1030 Brussels
Tel : (32) (2) 735-0971
Fax : (32) (2) 732-2022
Patricia Kelly

CNN (Spanish Program)
Avenue de l'Hippodrome, 93
B - 1050 Brussels
Tel : (32) (2) 646-3354
Fax : (32) (2) 646-3354
Marcela Szymanski Chave

Eurowatch
Square Ambiorix, 51
B - 1040 Brussels
Tel : (32) (2) 230-8137
Fax : (32) (2) 736-3162
Elizabeth Greathouse

International Herald Tribune
Rue Vergote, 32
B - 1200 Brussels
Tel : (32) (2) 735-4476
Fax : (32) (2) 735-8909
Thomas Buerkle

Knight-Ridder Financial News
IPC Bd Charlemagne, 1 - Bte 14
B - 1041 Brussels
Tel : (32) (2) 238-1457
Tel : (32) (2) 231-1450
Fax : (32) (2) 230-0518
David Thomas
Marlee Van Parys

Market News Service
Rue Philippe Le Bon, 15
B - 1040 Brussels
Tel : (32) (2) 230-0409
Fax : (32) (2) 230-0409
Kevin Woodfield

Middle East International
Rue Philippe Le Bon, 15
B - 1000 Brussels
Tel : (32) (2) 230-4267
Fax : (32) (2) 230-4267
Shadaba Islam

Multichannel News
Rue Américaine, 19
B - 1050 Brussels
Tel : (32) (2) 534-3966
John Grant

New York Journal of Commerce
IPC - Bd Charlemagne, 1
B - 1041 Brussels
Tel : (32) (2) 540-9090
Fax : (32) (2) 540-9093
Fax : (32) (2) 540-9070
Bruce Barnard
Peter Dreyer (32) (2) 734-7842

Newsweek
Rue Guillaume Stocq, 48
B - 1050 Brussels
Tel : (32) (2) 649-3346
Dorinda Elliott

Niagara Television Ltd
Trèves Center - Rue de Trèves, 45
B - 1040 Brussels
Tel : (32) (2) 238-7862
Fax : (32) (2) 238-7700
Jonathan Kapstein

Time Magazine
Bd Brand Whitlock, 42
B - 1200 Brussels
Tel : (32) (2) 735-4242
Fax : (32) (2) 735-9269
Fax : (32) (2) 735-4919
James A. Branegan
Catherine Kotschouby (32)(2) 735-3972
John Wyles

UPI
IPC - Bd Charlemagne, 1 - Bte 64
B - 1041 Brussels
Tel : (32) (2) 230-4330
Fax : (32) (2) 230-4381
Lucius Hill

US News & World Report
Treves Center - Rue de Trèves, 45
B-1040 Brussels
Tel : (32) (2) 238-7862
Jonathan Kapstein

Variety
Rue des Patriotes, 35
B - 1000 Brussels
Tel : (32) (2) 733-5769
Fax : (32) (2) 732-9325
Andrew Stern

Wall Street Journal
Bd Brand Whitlock, 87
B - 1200 Brussels
Tel : (32) (2) 741-1326
Tel : (32) (2) 741-1327
Tel : (32) (2) 741-1325

Tel : (32) (2) 741-1324
Fax : (32) (2) 741-1601
Fax : (32) (2) 741-1600
Brian Coleman
Charles Goldsmith
Shailagh Murray
James Terence Roth (Bureau Chief)

Wall Street Journal Europe
Rue Philippe Le Bon, 15
B - 1040 Brussels
Tel : (32) (2) 230-9800
Fax : (32) (2) 230-8776
Julie Wolf

Wordservice International
Rue de l'Espagne, 12
B-1000 Brussels
Tel : (32) (2) 218-6830
Fax : (32) (2) 230-8009

ALPHABETICAL LISTING OF
ACCREDITED JOURNALISTS
TO THE EU WORKING FOR US MEDIA

As of the date of this publication, there are 41 journalists accredited to the EU working for US Media.

PA = Press Agency, WP= Written Press, AV= Audio-Visual

Paul David Ames	Associated Press (PA)
Bruce Barnaard	New York Journal of Commerce (WP)
Linda Bernier	Business Week (WP)
James A. Branegan	Time Magazine (WP)
Thomas Buerkle	International Herald Tribune (WP)
Raf Casert	Associated Press (PA)
Claude Colart	Associated Press (PA)
Brian Coleman	The Wall Street Journal (WP)
Elizabeth De Bony	Business International (WP)
	IPG News Service
Peter Dreyer	New York Journal of Commerce (WP)
William Echikson	Business Week (WP)
Dorinda Elliott	Newsweek (WP)
Charles Goldsmith	Wall Street Journal (WP)
Peter Goldstein	AP-Dow Jones (PA)
Elizabeth Greathouse	Eurowatch (WP)
Stephanie Griffith	Associated Press (PA)
Caroline Jacobs	Bloomberg Busines News (PA)
Martin Jay	Wordservice International (PA)
Jonathan Kapstein	US News & World Report (WP)
Patricia Kelly	CNN (Cable News Network) (AV)
Claudia Kemmer	Associated Press (German Service) (PA)
James Joseph Kirwin	Bureau of National Affairs (WP)
Catherine Kotschoubey	Time Magazine (WP)
Grainne Mc Carthy	AP-Dow Jones (PA)
Robert Mc Leod	Bloomberg News (PA)
Raphael Minder	Bloomberg Business News (PA)
Shailagh Murray	The Wall Street Journal (WP)
James Neuger	Bloomberg Business News (PA)
James Terence Roth	Wall Street Journal (WP)
Koenrad Santersman	Associated Press (PA)

Jonathan Stearns	AP-Dow Jones (PA)
Andrew Stern	Variety (WP)
	Business Europe (WP)
Marcela Szymanski Chave	CNN (Spanish Program) (AV)
David Thomas	Bridge News (PA)
David W. Tweed	AP-Doiw Jones (PA)
Jeffrey Ulbrich	Associated Press (PA)
Marleen Van Parys	Bridge News (PA)
Robert J. Wielaard	Associated Press (PA)
Julie Wolf	Wall Street Journal (WP)
Kevin Woodfield	Market News Service (PA)
John Wyles	Time Magazine (WP)

ACCREDITED JOURNALISTS
TO THE EU WORKING FOR US MEDIA

Name & Address   **US Media**

Paul David Ames   Associated Press
IPC - Bd Charlemagne, 1
Bte 49
B - 1041 Brussels
Tel : (32) (2) 285-0130/31
Fax : (32) (2) 285-0155

Bruce Barnard   New York Journal
IPC-Bd. Charlemagne, 1   of Commerce
B-1041 Brussels
Tel : (32) (2) 540-9090
Fax : (32 (2) 540-9093

Linda Bernier   Business Week
Avenue de Floride, 118
B - 1180 Brussels
Tel : (32) (2) 375-7016
Fax : (32) (2) 374-3426

James A. Branegan   Time Magazine
Bd Brand Whitlock, 42
B - 1200 Brussels
Tel : (32) (2) 735-4242
Fax : (32) (2) 735-9269

Thomas Buerkle   International
Rue Vergote, 32   Herald Tribune
B - 1200 Brussels
Tel : (32) (2) 735-4476
Fax : (32) (2) 735-8909

Raf Casert   Associated Press
IPC-Boulevard Charlemagne, 1
Bte 49
B-1041 Brussels
Tel : (32) (2) 285-0112
Fax : (32) (2) 285-0155

Claude Colart   Associated Press
IPC-Boulevard Charlemagne, 1
Bte 49
B-1041 Brussels
Tel : (32) (2) 285-0112
Fax : (32) (2) 285-0155

Brian Coleman   The Wall Street Journal
Bd Brand Whitlock, 87
B - 1200 Brussels
Tel : (32) (2) 741-1326
Fax : (32) (2) 741-1601

Elizabeth De Bony   Business International
Avenue George Henri, 2
B-1200 Brussels
Tel : (32) (2) 223-0495
Fax : (32) (2) 271-4102

Peter Dryer   New York Journal of Commerce
IPC-Boulevard Charlemagne, 1
B-1041 Brussels
Tel : (32) (2) 540-9090
Fax : (32) (2) 540-9093

William Echikson   Business Week
Avenue de la Floride, 118
B-1180 Brussels
Tel : (32) (2) 375-7016
Fax : (32) (2) 374-3426

Dorina Elliott
Rue Guillaume Stocq
B - 1050 Brussels
Tel : (32) (2) 649-3346

Newsweek

Charles Goldsmith
Boulevard Brand Whitlock, 87
B-1200 Brussels
Tel : (32) (2) 741-1326
Fax : (32) (2) 741-1601

Wall Street Journal

Peter Goldstein
IPC - Bd Charlemagne, 1
Bte 49
B - 1041 Brussels
Tel : (32) (2) 285-0130
Fax : (32) (2) 285-0156

AP Dow Jones

Elizabeth Greathouse
Square Ambiorix, 51
B-1040 Brussels
Tel : (32) (2) 230-8137
Fax : (32) (2) 736-3162

Eurowatch

Stephanie Griffith
IPC -Boulevard Charlemagne, 1
Bte 49
B-1041 Brussels
Tel : (32) (2) 285-0112
Fax : (32) (2) 285-0155

Associated Press

Caroline Jacobs
IPC- Boulevard Charlemagne, 1
B-1041 Brussels
Tel : (32) (2) 280-0126
Fax : (32) (2) 230-2514

Bloomberg Business News

Martin Jay   Wordservice International
Rue de l'Espagne, 12
B-1000 Brussels
Tel : (32) (2) 218-6830
Fax : (32) (2) 230-8009

Jonathan Kapstein   US News &
Rue de Trèves, 45   World Report
B - 1040 Brussels
Tel : (32) (2) 238-78-62
Fax : (32) (2) 238-7700
E-mail: 100433.1117@compuserve.com

Patricia Kelly   CNN
Chaussée de Louvain, 515   (Cable News
B - 1030 Brussels   Network)
Tel : (32) (2) 735-0971
Fax : (32) (2) 732-2022

Claudia Kemmer   Associated Press
Boulevard Charlemagne, 1   (German Service)
Bte 49
B-1040 Brussels
Tel : (32) (2) 285-0115
Fax : (32) (2) 285-0155

James Joseph Kirwin   Bureau of National Affairs
Rue des Platanes, 39
B-1040 Brussels
Tel : (32) (2) 732-3740

Catherine Kotschoubey   Time Magazine
Boulevard Brand Whitlock, 42
B-1200 Brussels
Tel : (32) (2) 735-4242
Fax : (32) (2) 735-9269

Grainne Mc Carthy
IPC-Boulevard Charlemagne, 1
Bte 49
B-1041 Brussels
Tel : (32) (2) 285-0130
Fax : (32) (2) 285-0156

AP-Dow Jones

Robert Mc Leod
IPC- Boulevard Charlemagne, 1
Bte 28
B-1041 Brussels
Tel : (32) (2) 285-4300
Fax : (32) (2) 285-4303

Bloomberg News

Raphael Minder
IPC-Boulevard Charlemagne, 1
B-1041 Brussels
Tel : (32) (2) 280-0126
Fax : (32) (2) 280-2514

Bloomberg Business News

Shailagh Murray
Boulevard Brand Whitlock, 87
B-1200 Brussels
Tel : (32) (2) 741-1326
Fax : (32) (2) 741-1600

The Wall Street Journal

James Neuger
IPC-Boulevard Charlemagne, 1
Bte 28
B-1041 Brussels
Tel : (32) (2) 285-4300
Fax : (32) (2) 285-4303

Bloomberg Business News

James Terence Roth
Boulevard Brand Whitlock, 87
B-1200 Brussels
Tel : (32) (2) 741-1326
Fax : (32) (2) 741-1601

Wall Street Journal

Koenrad Santersman   Associated Press
IPC-Boulevard Charlemagne, 1
B-1041 Brussels
Tel : (32) (2) 285-0112
Fax : (32) (2) 285-0155

Jonathan Stearns   AP- Dow Jones
IPC-Boulevard Charlemagne, 1
B-1041 Brussels
Tel : (32) (2) 285-0130
Fax : (32) (2) 285-0156

Marcela Szymanski Chave   CNN (Spanish Program)
Avenue de l'Hippodrome, 93
B - 1030 Brussels
Tel : (32) (2) 646-3354 (PRV)
Fax : (32) (2) 646-3354 (PRV)

David Thomas   Bride News
IPC- Boulevard Charlemagne, 1
Bte 14
B-1041 Brussels
Tel: (32) (2) 231-1450
Fax: (32) (2) 230-0518

David W. Tweed   AP-Dow Jones
IPC-Boulevard Charlemagne, 1
B-1041 Brussels
Tel : (32) (2) 285-0132
Fax : (32) (2) 285-0156

Jeffrey Ulbrich   Associated Press
IPC-Boulevard Charlemagne, 1
Bte 49
B-1041 Brussels
Tel : (32) (2) 285-0112
Fax : (32) (2) 285-0155

Marleen Van Parys
IPC-Boulevard Charlemagne, 1
Bte 14
B-1041 Brussels
Tel : (32) (2) 231-1450
Fax : (32) (2) 230-0518

Bridge News

Robert J; Wielaard
IPC-Boulevard Charlemagne, 1
Bte 49
B-1041 Brussels
Tel : (32) (2) 285-0112
Fax : (32) (2) 285-0155

Associated Press

Julie Wolf
Boulevard Brand Whitlock, 87
B-1200 Brussels
Tel : (32) (2) 230-9800
Fax : (32) (2) 230-8776

Wall Street Journal

Kevin Woodfield
Rue Philippe Le Bon, 15
B-1040 Brussels
Tel : (32) (2) 230-0409
Fax : (32) (2) 230-0409

Markzet News Service

John Wyles
Boulevard Brand Whitlock, 42
B-1200 Brussels
Tel : (32) (2) 735-4242
Fax : (32) (2) 735-9269

Time Magazine

CHAPTER 15
MAJOR US CORPORATE
REPRESENTATIONS TO THE EU

Many US corporations have established full-time European Public Affairs Directors, or have executives with other titles who deal regularly in the field of Government/Public Affairs. They may provide valuable tips about the functioning of the Commission and pitfalls to avoid when establishing a presence in Brussels.

The list hereafter is not exhaustive.

Company

3 M Europe
Hermeslaan, 7
B-1831 Diegem
Tel : (32) (2) 722-4500
Fax : (32) (2) 722-4511
Public Affairs Contact Person : Mr.Rowen
Title: Public Affairs Manager Europe
Sector of Activity: Communication / Construction / Pharmaceuticals / Industry / Office, Automation / Health Care / Electronics / Electrical Products / Automotive / Personnel and Traffic Safety

Abbott
Rue du Bosquet, 2
B-1348 Louvain-La-Neuve
Tel : (32) (10) 47-53-11
Fax : (32) (10).47-55-75
Public Affairs Contact Person : Mr. Jean-Loup Rolland
Title: General Manager
Sector of Activity : Health Care/Pharmaceuticals

Air Products
Chaussée de Wavre, 1789
B-1160 Brussels
Tel : (32) (2)674-9411
Fax : (32) (2) 674-9462
Public Affairs Contact Person : Mr. Daniel Galle
Title: Marketing Communication & PR Manager Europe
Sector of Activity: Industrial Gazes / Specialty Gazes / Related Equipment

Allied Signal Europe SA
Haasrode Research Park
Grauwmeer, 1
B-3001 Leuven
Tel : (32) (16) 39-13-00
Fax : (32) (16) 40-08-74
Public Affairs Contact Person: Mrt. M.HJ. Wilson
Title: Managing Director
Sector of Activity: Engineered Materials / Engineered Plastics / Specialty
                       Films / Specialty Chemichals / Fluorine Products

American Airlines
Rue du Trône, 98
B-1050 Brussels
Tel : (32) (2) 508-7700
Fax : (32) (2) 508-7800
Public Affairs Contact Person : Mr.Joseph Le Pochat
Title: Director Government Affairs
Sector of Activity : Air Transport

Amoco Services
Amoco House, West Gate
GB-London W5 1 XL
Tel : 44/181/991-5639
Fax : 44/181/849-7329
Public Affairs Contact Person: Mr. Neil Chapman
Title: Head of Public Affairs
Public Affairs Contact Person : Mr. Harry MacMillan
Title: Managing Director International Government & Public Affairs
Sector of Activity: Energy/ Natural Gas/ Oil Production

Amway (Europe)
Avenue des Arts, 50 - Bte 18
B-1000 Brussels
Tel : (32) (2) 514-0010
Fax : (32) (2) 514-2242
Public Affairs Contact Person : Mr. Al Koop
Title: Managing Director
Public Affairs Contact Person: Mrs. Bettina Ungerer
Title: Legal Counsel, EU Government Affairs
Sector of Activity: Health Care/Pharmaceuticals

Andlinger & Co
Avenue Louise, 148 - Bte 2
B-1050 Brussels
Tel : (32) (2) 647-8070
Fax : (32) (2) 647-2105
Public Affairs Contact Person: Mr. Johan Volckaerts
Title: President Europe
Sector of Activity: Mergers & Acquisitions

Apple Computer Europe
Corporate Affairs
Bureau Design Center
Esplanade Heysel Bte 100
B-1020 Brussels
Tel : (32) (2) 474-4390
Fax : (32) (2) 474-4304
Public Affairs Contact Person: Mrs. Josiane Morel
Title: EU Corporate Manager
Sector of Activity: Computers/Hi-Tech

Arco Chemical Europe
Trèves Center
Rue de Trèves, 45
B-1040 Brussels
Tel : (32) (2) 238-7862
Fax : (32) (2) 238-7714
Public Affairs Contact Person: Mr. Jonathan Kapstein
Title: Director Government Relations
Sector of Activity: Chemical Industry

AT& T Communications Services
Chaussée de Wavre, 1945
B-1160 Brussels
Tel : (32) (2) 676-3556
Fax : (32) (2) 676-3807
Public Affairs Contact Person: Mr. Harry U. Elhardt
Title: Director EU Public Affairs
Sector of Activity: Telecommunications

Avon European Affairs
Avenue Lambeau, 38
B-1200 Brussels
Tel : (32) (2) 733-5919
Fax : (32) (2) 734-6742
Public Affairs Contact Person: Mr. Raymond Verbeugt
Title: Adviser European Affairs
Sector of Activity : Cosmetics / Beauty Products

Baxter World Trade
Rue Colonel Bourg, 105B
B-1140 Brussels
Tel : (32) (2) 702-1711
Fax : (32) (2) 702-1634
Public Affairs Contact Person: Mr. Jean-Marie Vlassembrouck
Title: Vice-President Public Affairs
Sector of Activity: Health Care/Pharmaceuticals

Bristol-Myers Squibb
Waterloo Office park - Drève Richelle, 161
B-1410 Waterloo
Tel : (32) (2) 352-7411
Fax : (32) (2) 352-7383
Public Affairs Contact Person: Mr. A. Hoefmans
Title: Vice-President Government & Corporate Affairs Europe
Sector of Activity: Health Care/Pharmaceuticals/Nutritional

Browning-Ferris Industries Europe - (BFIE)
Avenue d'Auderghem, 150
B-1040 Brussels
Tel : (32) (2) 732-5040
Fax : (32) (2) 736-0506
Public Affairs Contact Person: Mrs. Jane Mc Kay
Title: Government Affairs Representative
Sector of Activity: Services Industry/Waste management

Cabot Plastics International
Interleuvenlaan, 5
B-3001 Leuven
Tel : (32) (16) 39-01-11
Fax : (32) (16) 40-12-53
Public Affairs Contact Person: Mr. Gerard Romainville
Title: Communications Manager
Sector of Activity: Chemicals Industry

Campbell Coordination Center
Belgicastraat, 3
B-1930 Zaventem
Tel : (32) (2) 718-3311
Fax : (32) (2) 718-3541
Public Affairs Contact Person: Mrs. Ingrid Baeten
Title: Legal Counsel
Sector of Activity : Food Products

Cargill Europe
Knowle Hill Park-Fairmile Lane
GB-Cobham, Surrey KT 11 2PD
Tel : (44) (1932) 861-000
Fax : (44) (1932) 861-264
Public Affairs Contact Person: Ms. Ruth Rawling
Title: Director, European Government Affairs
Sector of Activity: Agriculture / Fisheries / Banking / Financial / Services /
                        Drink Industry / Food

Caterpillar Group Services
Chaussée de la Hulpe, 130
B-1000 Brussels
Tel : (32) (2) 672-1740
Fax : (32) (2) 672-0803
Public Affairs Contact Person: Mr. William W. Beddow
Title: Director Public Affairs Europe
Sector of Activity: Agriculture / Earthmoving Equipment / Banking /
                       Financial Services / Construction / Energy / Utilities

Chevron UK
Portman Street 2
GB-London W1H OAN
Tel : (44) (171) 487-8100
Fax : (44) (171) 487-8770
Public Affairs Contact Person: Mr. Simon Lowes
Title: Government Public Affairs Manager
Sector: Energy / Utilities / Chemical Industry

Chrysler Europe
Boulevard de la Woluwe, 106-108
B-1200 Brussels
Tel : (32) (2) 775-4211
Fax : (32) (2) 775-4460
Public Affairs Contact Person: Mr. Han Tjan
Title: Manager
Sector of Activity: Automotive

Citibank
Boulevard Genéral Jacques, 263g
B-1050 Brussels
Tel : (32) (2) 626-5111
Fax : (32) (2) 626-5584
Public Affairs Contact Person:Mr. Sandy Vaci
Title: Marketing
Sector of Activity: Banking

Coca Cola Greater Europe
Chaussée de Mons, 1424
B-1070 Brussels
Tel : (32) (2) 529-1701
Fax : (32) (2) 529-1851
Public Affairs Contact Person: Mr. Walter Brinkmann
Title: Senior Vice-President EU Affairs
Sector of Activity: Drink Industry / Food

Colgate Palmolive Belgium/Europe
Boulevard de la Woluwe, 58
B-1200 Brussels
Tel : (32) (2) 761-5211
Fax : (32) (2) 761-5208
Public Affairs Contact Person: Mrs. Bernadette Doumont
Title: Public Affairs
Sector of Activity: Public Affairs

Compaq Computer
Lozenberg, 17
B-1932 Zaventem
Tel : (32) (2) 716-9511
Fax : (32) (2) 725-2213
Public Affairs Contact Person: Mr. Dominique Demey
Title: Marketing Services Manager
Sector of Activity: Computers / high-Tech

Corning Europe
c/o G.H; Besselaar Associates
Avenue de Tervuren, 273
B-1150 Brussels
Tel : (32) (2) 773-2911
Fax : (32) (2) 772-2998
Public Affairs Contact Person: Mr. Pierre-Louis Roederer
Title: Vice-President & Director Government Affairs Europe
Sector of Activity: Specialty Glass and Ceramics / Environmental and
Telecommunications Products

CPC Europe Consumer Foods
Avenue de Tervuren, 300 - Bte 7
B-1150 Brussels
Tel : (32) (2) 761-0948
Fax : (32) (2) 761-0918
Public Affairs Contact Person: Mr. Ernst Rapp
Title: Director Food Law & Safety
Sector of Activity: Food

Cyanamid International
Rue du Bosquet, 15
B-1348 Louvain-La-Neuve
Tel : (32) (10) 49-37-36
Fax : (32) (10) 49-48-00
Public Affairs Contact Person: Dr. David Baldwin
Title: Regional Technical Director
Sector of Activity: Pharmaceuticals

DHL Worldwide Express
Rue Colonel Bourg, 124
B-1140 Brussels
Tel : (32) (2) 730-1811
Fax : (32) (2) 730-8699
Public Affairs Contact Person: Mr. Roland Steisel
Title: Director Legal & Regulatory Affairs & Administration
Sector of Activity:Express Delivery Service

Digital Equipment Corporation
Rue de l'Aéronef, 1
B-1140 Brussels
Tel : (32) (2) 729-8219
Fax : (32) (2) 729-8235
Public Affairs Contact Person: Mrs. Salies Crenshaw
Title: Director EU & Government Relations
Sector of Activity: Computers / High-Tech

Donaldson Europe N.V.
Interleuvenlaan 1
B-3001 Leuven
Tel : (32) (16) 383811
Fax : (32) (16) 400077
Public Affairs Contact Person : Mr Geert Henk Touw
Title : Managing Director
Sector of Activity : Filtration

Dow Corning
Coordination Center
Rue du Général de Gaulle, 62
B-1310 La Hulpe
Tel : (32) (2) 655-2099
Fax : (32) (2) 655-2005
Public Affairs Contact Person : Mr. Alain Joachim
Title: Vice-President
Sector of Activity: Silicon Manufacturers

Dow Europe
Rue de Trèves, 45
B-1040 Brussels
Tel : (32) (2) 238-7838
Fax : (32) (2) 238-7731
Public Affairs Contact Person: Mrs. Geneviève De Bauw
Title: Director of EU Government Affairs
Sector of Activity: Chemicals Industry

Dresser Europe
Boulevard du Souverain, 191-197 - Bte 3
B-1160 Brussels
Tel : (32) (2) 660-2060
Fax : (32) (2) 660-1682
Public Affairs Contact Person: Mr. Patrick Foley
Title: Delegate
Sector of Activity: Oil Field Services

Dupont de Nemours International
Chemin du Pavillon 2
CH-1218 Le Grand Saconnex/GE
Tel : (41) (22) 717-5270
Fax : (41)(22).717-6077
Public Affairs Contact Person: Mr. Ursus Jaeggi
Title: Director Government Affairs Europe
Sector of Activity: Chemicals Industry

Eastman Kodak
Steenstraat 20
B-1800 Koningslo Vilvoorde
Tel : (32) (2) 263-2709
Fax : (32) (2) 263-2704
Public Affairs Contact Person: Mr. Bengt Ekelund
Title: Director European Affairs
Sector of Activity: Chemical Industry / Computers, High Tech / Health Care
                       / Services Industry / Telecommunications / Imaging,
                       Photography

EDS-Electronic Data Systems
Fountain Plaza
Belgicastraat, 5
B-1930 Zaventem
Tel : (32) (2) 716-3833
Fax : (32) (2) 716-3760
Public Affairs Contact Person: Mr. Brian Maitland -Reynell
Title: Director, Government Affairs Europe
Public Affairs Contact Person: Mr. Martyn Lowry
Title: Director European Public Affairs
Sector of Activity: Electronics / Information Technology Services

Eli-Lilly Benelux
Rue de L'Etuve, 52 - Bte 1
B-1000 Brussels
Tel : (32) (2) 548-8500
Fax : (32) (2) 502-1355
Public Affairs Contact Person: DR. Marc Czarka
Title: Director Corporate Affairs
Sector of Activity: Health Care / Pharmaceuticals

Enron Europe
Four Millbank
GB-London SW1P 3 ET
Tel : (44) (171) 316-5480
Fax : (44) (171) 316-5391
Public Affairs Contact Person: Mr. Peter R; Styles
Title: Vicve-President EU Government Affairs
Public Affairs Contact Person: Mr. Mark Schroeder
Title: Vice-President Regulatory Affairs
Sector of Activity: Energy / Utilities / Banking / Financial Services

Exxon Chemical Europe
Boulevard du Souverain, 280
B-1160 Brussels
Tel : (32) (2) 674-4111
Fax : (32) (2) 674-4129
Public Affairs Contact Person: Dr. Basil Zirius
Title: Vice-President EU Affairs
Public Affairs Contact Person: Mr. Marcel Daniels
Title: Manager Public Affairs Europe
Sector of Activity: Chemical Indusrtry

Federal Express
Airport Building, 119
B-1820 Melsbroek
Tel : (32) (2) 752-7248
Fax : (32) (2) 752-7262
Public Affairs Contact Person: Mr. Ricahrd Gerber
Title: Vice-President Regional Counsel
Sector of Activity: Services Industry / Transport / Air Transport / Document
                       / Packages Delivery / Freight

FMC Europe
Avenue Louise, 480 - Bte 9
B-1050 Brussels
Tel : (32) (2) 645-9211
Fax : (32) (2) 645-9401
Public Affairs Contact Person: Mr. Daniel J; Gachet
Title: General Counsel Europe
Sector of Activity: Chemical Industry / Drink Industry / Food / Packaging /
                       Health Care / Pharmaceuticals / Machinery / Equipment.

Ford of Europe
Boulevard de la Woluwe, 2 - Bte 4
B-1150 Brussels
Tel : (32) (2) 762-1070
Fax : (32) (2) 762-9564
Public Affairs Contact Person: Mr. Jan F. candries
Title: Director European Affairs
Sector of Activity: Automotive

General Electric International
Boulevard du Souverain, 165
B-1160 Brussels
Tel : (32) (2) 679-0150
Fax : (32) (2) 675-2754
Public Affairs Contact Person: Mrs. Anneliese Monden
Title: Manager, European Affairs Office
Sector of Activity: Energy / utilities

General Motors Coordination Center
Rue Neerveld, 107
B-1200 Brussels
Tel : (32) (2) 773-6983
Fax : (32) (2) 773-6930
Public Affairs Contact Person: Mr. Johan De Schrijver
Title: Managing Director
Public Affairs Contact Person: Mr. Peter von Manteuffel
Title: Executive Director
Sector of Activity: Automotive

Gillette Belgium
Rue Defacqs, 115
B-1060 Brussels
Tel : (32) (2) 537-0235
Fax : (32) (2) 539-3554
Public Affairs Contact Person: Mr. Christopher Adcock
Title: Managing Director
Sector of Activity: Toiletries Products

Goodyear Benelux
Spoorweglaan, 3
B-2610 Wilrijk
Tel : (32) (3) 820-3211
Fax : (32) (3) 820-3300
Public Affairs Contact Person: Mrs; Marijke Matthijs
Title: Advertising & PR Administrator
Sector of Activity: Tyres

Hercules Europe
Coordination Centre
Avenue de Tervuren, 300
B-1150 Brussels
Tel : (32) (2) 761-5511
Fax : (32) (2) 761-5555
Public Affairs Contact Person: Mr. Rick Gigbels
Title: Manager Administration
Sector of Activity: Chemical Industry

Hewlett Packard
Boulevard de la Woluwe, 100-102
B-1200 Brussels
Tel : (32) (2) 778-3939
Fax : (32) (2) 778-3938
Public Affairs Contact Person: Mr. Hans-Jochen Lueckefest
Title: Director, Government Affairs Europe
Public Affairs Contact Person: Mr. Gilles Polin
Title: Business Development Manager EU Programs
Sector of Activity : Computer Systems / Computer Products

H.J. Heinz Company
Hayes Park
GB-Hayes, Middlesex UB4 8AL
Tel : (44) (181) 848-2239
Fax : (44) (181) 848-2640
Public Affairs Contact Person: Mr. Nick Harding
Title: Managing Director, Northern Europe
Sector of Activity: Food Products

Honeywell Europe
Avenue du Bourget, 3
B-1140 Brussels
Tel : (32) (2) 728-2728
Fax : (32) (2) 728-2639
Public Affairs Contact Person: Mr. Bolko Nawrocki
Title: Vice-President of Business Development
Public Affairs Contact Person: Mr. Alessandro Profili
Title: Director Communication & Public Affairs
Sector of Activity: Process Management Systems for Environmental Protection / Energy, Conservation / Home Safety / Industry / Aviation / Space / Buildings

Hughes Electronics
c/o Hughes Europe
Avenue Ariane, 5
B-1200 Brussels
Tel : (32) (2) 778-4911
Fax : (32) (2) 778-4999
Public Affairs Contact Person : Mr. Paul Stefens
Title: Public Affairs Representative Europe
Sector of Activity: Aerospace / Air Transport / Automotive / Electronics / Computers / Hi-Tech / Telecommunications / Defense

IBM Europe, Middle East & Africa
Governmental Programs
Chaussée de Bruxelles, 135
B-1310 La Hulpe
Tel : (32) (2) 655-5337
Fax : (32) (2) 655-5300
Public Affairs Contact Person: Mr. Jean-Louis De Turckheim
Title: Vice-President
Public Affairs Contact Person: Mr. Gerd Kirchkoff
Title: Director
Sector of Activity: Electronics / Computers / Hi-Tech / Services Industry / Telecommunications

Intel Corporation
European Affairs Office
Avenue Winston Churchill, 11
B-1180 Brussels
Tel : (32) (2) 345-0028
Fax : (32) (2) 347-0585
Public Affairs Contact Person: Mrs. Monique Meche
Title: EU Affairs Manager
Sector of Activity: Electronic Components and Systems

International Paper Europe
Boulevard de la Woluwe, 100
B-1200 Brussels
Tel : (32) (2) 774-1236
Fax : (32) (2) 770-2337
Public Affairs Contact Person: Mr. Erik D. Lazar
Title: Senor Legal Counsel
Sector ofActivity: Paper / Forest Products / Imaging / Chemical Industry /
                      Packaging

Johnson & Johnson
European Office
Avenue des Arts, 46
B-1000 Brussels
Tel : (32) (2) 506-1111
Fax : (32) (2) 506-1161
Public Affairs Contact Person: Mr. John Mullin
Title: Public Affairs
Sector of Activity : Health Care Products

Kellogg Europe
Kellogg Building
Talbot Road
GB-Manchester M16 OPU
Tel : (44) (161) 869-2227
Fax : (44) (161) 869-2103
Public Affairs Contact Person: Mr. Neil Nyberg
Title: Director Corporate Affairs Europe
Sector of Activity: Food / Drink Industry

Kimberly Clark
Trèves Centre
Rue de Trèves
B-1040 Brussels
Tel : (32) (2) 238-7804
Fax : (32) (2) 238-7701
Public Affairs Contact Person : Mr. Barry J. Tubbs
Title : Vice President Europe Government Relations and Environmental Services
Sector of Activity : Household Paper Products

Lee Europe
Drève de Bonne Odeur, 20
B-1160 Brussels
Tel : (32) (2) 678-4311
Fax : (32) (2) 678-4344
Public Affairs Contact Person: Mr. Ron Mitchell
Title: President
Sector of Activity: Textiles

Levi Strauss Europe
Avenue Louise, 489
B-1050 Brussels
Tel : (32) (2) 641-6111
Fax : (32) (2) 641-6541
Public Affairs Contact Person: Mr. Jan Baszak
Title: Director Corporate Communication
Sector of Activity: Textiles

Mc Donald's Belgium
Vuurberg, 80
B-1831 Machelen
Tel : (32) (2) 716-0440
Fax : (32) (2) 716-0430
Public Affairs Contact Person: Mrs.Karen Van Bergen
Title: European Manager Government Relations
Sector of Activity: Food, Drink Industry

MCI International (Belgium)
Rue Colonel Bourg, 123-125
B-1140 Brussels
Tel : (32) (2) 706-6411
Fax : (32) (2) 706-6464
Public Affairs Contact Person: Mr. Roger D. Daem
Title: General Manager
Sector of Activity : Telecommunications

Merck Sharp & Dohme Europe
Clos du Lynx, 5
B-1200 Brussels
Tel : (32) (2) 776-6452
Fax : (32) (2) 776-6482
Public Affairs Contact Person: Mr. Charles Bouchard
Title: Sr. Director Europe Public Affairs
Sector of Activity: Pharmaceuticals

Mobil Europe EU Representation
Boulevard du Régent, 50 - Bte 2
B-1000 Brussels
Tel : (32) (2) 511-2248
Fax : (32) (2) 502-2898
Public Affairs Contact Person: Dr. Frank C. Völcker
Title: Director EU Relations
Public Affairs Contact Person: Mr. E.P. Goulley
Title: Senior Advisor
Sector of Activity: Energy / Petroleum

Monroe Europe
Rue A. De Boek, 56
B-1140 Brussels
Tel : (32) (2) 240-1411
Fax : (32) (2) 242-9637
Public Affairs Contact Person: Mrs. Dolores Muniz
Title: Public Relations Manager
Sector of Activity: Automotive

Monsanto Europe
Avenue de Tervuren, 270-270
B-1150 Brussels
Tel : (32) (2) 776-4111
Fax : (32) (2) 776-4040
Public Affairs Contact Person: Dr. Kenneth M. Baker
Title: Director Government Affairs
Public Affairs Contact Person: Mr. Thomas J. Mc Dermott
Title: Head of Public Affairs
Sector of Activity: Chemical Industry

Morgan Stanley Group (Europe)
Cabot Square 25
Canary Wharf
GB-London E14 1QA
Tel : (44) (171) 425-4940
Fax : (44) (171) 425-4949
Public Affairs Contact Person: Mrs. Amelia C. Fawcett
Title: Executive Director
Sector of Activity: Investment Banking

NCR Europe
Rue de la Fusée, 50
B-1130 Brussels
Tel : (32) (2) 727-9211
Fax : (32) (2) 727-9288
Public Affairs Contact Person: Mr. Mike Buchanan
Title: Director European Institutions
Sector of Activity: Computers / Hi-Tech

Northrop Gruman International
Avenue de Broqueville, 12 - Bte 8
B-1150 Brussels
Tel : (32) (2) 772-0409
Fax : (32) (2) 771-6217
Public Affairs Contact Person: Mr. Thomas F. Darcy
Title: Managing Director, European Region
Sector of Activity: Electronics / Aerospace / Air Transport

Novus Europe
Rue Gulledelle, 94
B-1200 Brussels
Tel : (32) (2) 778-1411
Fax : (32) (2) 771-8287
Public Affairs Contact Person: Mr. Alain Brudichau
Title: Marketing Manager
Sector of Activity: Chemicals / Feed Additives for Animals

Nynex
Research Park Kranenberg
B-1731 Zellik
Tel : (32) (2) 463-3201
Fax : (32) (2) 463-1706
Public Affairs Contact Person: Ms. Karen Corbett Sanders
Title: Regional Director Government Affairs
Sector of Activity: Telecommunications

Occidental Chemical Europe
Henry Fordlaan, 80
B-3600 Genk
Tel : (32) (89) 35-49-11
Fax : (32) (89) 36-32-02
Public Affairs Contact Person: Mr. A. Dankers
Title: General Manager
Sector of Activity: Chemical Industry

Owens Corning
Chaussée de la Hulpe, 178
B-1170 Brussels
Tel : (32) (2) 674-8211
Fax : (32) (2) 675-266
Public Affairs Contact Person: Mrs. Martine Ledin
Title: Marketing & Communication Manager
Sector of Activity: Fiber Glass

Pennzoil Company
Place Tomberg, 8 - Bte 12
B-1200 Brussels
Tel : (32) (2) 779-2015
Fax : (32) (2) 772-9302
Public Affairs Contact Person: Mrs. Margaret O'Donnell
Title: EU Liaison
Sector of Activity: Energy / Petroleum Products

Perkin-Elmer
Leuvensesteenweg 510 - Box 5
B-1930 Zaventem
Tel : (32) (2) 712-5530
Fax : (32) (2) 725-4481
Public Affairs Contact Person: Mr. Willy Stelzer
Title: EC Business Coordinator
Sector of Activity: Analytic Equipment

Pfizer
Hoge Wei, 10
B-1930 Zaventem
Tel : (32) (2) 722-0265
Fax : (32) (2) 725-8628
Public Affairs Contact Person: Mr. Philip Hodger
Title: Executive Director, Corporate Affairs Europe
Public Affairs Contact Person: Ms. Eva Grut
Title: Director, Public Affairs Europe
Sector of Activity: Biotechnology / Health Care / Pharmaceuticals /
                       Veterinary Health Care

Philipps Petroleum Chemicals
Brusselsesteenweg, 355
B-3090 Overijse
Tel : (32) (2) 689-1220
Fax : (32) (2) 689-1472
Public Affairs Contact Person: Mrs. Yolande De Busschop
Title: Legal Director
Sector of Activity: Chemical Industry

Procter & Gamble
Temselaan, 100
B-1853 Strombeck-Bever
Tel : (32) (2) 456-2111
Fax : (32) (2) 456-2222
Public Affairs Contact Person: Mr. David E. Veitch
Title: Vice-President, Public Affairs Europe, Middle East & Africa
Sector of Activity: Chemical Industry / Detergents

Reynolds Consumer Europe
Otto De Mentock Plein, 19
B-1853 Strombeck-Bever
Tel : (32) (2) 263-5711
Fax : (32) (2) 267-9252
Public Affairs Contact Person: Mr. Kris van Gucht
Title: Marketing Manager
Sector of Activity: Aluminium Pipe

R.J. Reynolds International (RJRI)
Avenue Louise, 375 - Bte 10
B-1050 Brussels
Tel : (32) (2) 626-2470
Fax : (32) (2) 644-4600
Public Affairs Contact Person: Mr. Wilfried Dembach
Title: Vice-President Government Relations
Public Affairs Contact Person: Mr. Mark Arnauts
Director: Director, European Union Affairs
Sector of Activity: Tobacco

Rohm & Haas
Lennig House
Mason's Avenue 2
GB-Croydon CR9 3NB, Surrey
Tel : (44) (181) 686-8844
Fax : (44) (181) 680-7907
Public Affairs Contact Person: Mr. Mark Long
Title: European Public Affairs Manager
Sector of Activity: Chemical Industry

Raychem
Diestsesteenweg, 692
B-3010 Kessel-Lo
Tel : (32) (16) 35-10-11
Fax : (32) (16) 35-16-96
Public Affairs Contact Person: Mr. Eric Van Zele
Title: Managing Director
Sector of Activity: Chemicals

Smithkline Beecham
Avenue Louise, 287 - Bte 13
B-1050 Brussels
Tel : (32) (2) 640-8464
Fax : (32) (2) 648-5013
Public Affairs Contact Person: Mr. David J. Earnshaw
Title: Director EU Affairs
Sector of Activity: Pharmaceuticals

Tandem Computers
Lozenberg, 22
B-1932 Zaventem
Tel : (32) (2) 716-5211
Fax : (32) (2) 716-5210
Public Affairs Contact Person: Mr. Hans-Weenen
Title: Managing Director
Public Affairs Contact Person: Mrs Marijke Schross
Title: Marketing Communication
Sector of Activity : Computers / Hi-Tech

Texaco Services (Europe)
Avenue Arnaud Fraiteur, 25
B-1050 Brussels
Tel : (32) (2) 639-9111
Fax : (32) (2) 639-9222
Public Affairs Contact Person: Mr. Jaap Meinema
Title: Director EU & Government Affairs
Public Affairs Contact Person: Mrs. Susan Russell
Title: EU Affairs Manager
Sector Of Activity: Chemical Industry / Energy / Utilities

Texas Instruments
Avenue Jules Bordet, 11
B-1140 Brussels
Tel : (32) (2) 745-5400
Fax : (32) (2) 745-5410
Public Affairs Contact Person: Mr. Thomas Frankl
Title: Director, European Government Relations
Sector of Activity: Computers / Hi-Tech

Time Warner Europe
Boulevard Brand Whitlock, 42
B-1200 Brussels
Tel : (32) (2) 735-4242
Fax : (32) (2) 735-4034
Public Affairs Contact Person: Mr. Ivan Hodac
Title: Senior Vice-President
Sector of Activity: Audiovisual / Publishing / Media / Telecommunications
                      / Communication

TRW Systems Overseas
Avenue Franklin D. Roosevelt, 12
B-1050 Brussels
Tel : (32) (2) 640-0585
Fax : (32) (2) 640-1338
Public Affairs Contact Person: Mr. Frank Wieman
Title: Managing Director Europe
Sector of Activity: Aerospace / Air Transport / Automotive / Electronics /
                      Telecommunications

Union carbide (Europe)
Rue du Pré-Bouvier, 7
CH-1217 Meyrin
Tel : (41) (22) 989-6111
Fax : (41) (22) 989-6545
Public Affairs Contact Person: Mr. J.E. Stokoe
Title: Managing Director
Public Affairs Contact Person: Mr. W. Bracke
Title: Area Attorney
Sector of Activity: Chemical Industry

Unisys Europe
Avenue du Bourget, 20
B-1130 Brussels
Tel : (32) (2) 728-0711
Fax : (32) (2) 728-0409
Public Affairs Contact Person: Mrs. Dominique Sottiaux
Title: European Affairs Manager
Sector of Activity: Hardware and Software Products Specialized Systems

United Parcel Services
Woluwelaan, 158
B-1831 Diegem
Tel : (32) (2) 706-2807
Fax : (32) (2) 247-2940
Public Affairs Contact Person: Mr. Can Baki
Title: General Manager
Public Affairs Contact Person: Mrs Catherine Stuyck
Title: Public Relations Manager
Sector of Activity : Carrier Service

Upjohn
Rijksweg, 12
B-2870 Puurs
Tel: (32) (3) 890-9211
Fax: (32) (3) 889-6532
Public Affairs Contact Person: Mr. Frans Wauters
Title: Manager, Government Affairs
Public Affairs Contact Person: Mr. Jan H. Vijver
Title: Regional Public Manager Europe
Sector of Activity: Pharmaceuticals / Chemicals

Walt Disney Company (Benelux)
Boulevard Leopold II, 184D
B-1080 Brussels
Tel : (32) (2) 411-5656
Fax : (32)(2) 411-5554
Public Affairs Contact Person: Mr. Didier Vanneste
Title: Managing Director
Sector of Activity: Publishing / Licensing / Music

Warner-Lambert Belgium
Excelsiorlaan, 75-77
B-1930 Zaventem
Tel : (32) (2) 722-9111
Fax : (32) (2) 722-9102
Public Affairs Contact Person: Mr. Bernd Kolling
Title: General Director
Public Affairs Contact Person: Mrs; Annie Hubert
Title: Regulatory Affairs Manager
Sector of Activity: Pharmaceuticals

Waste Management International (WMI)
Avenue de Tervuren, 13
B-1040 Brussels
Tel : (32) (2) 732-3935
Fax : (32) (2) 732-6825
Public Affairs Contact Person: Mr. Wiliam Seddon-Brown
Title: Director, European Government Affairs
Sector of Activity: Waste Management / Transport / Water / Energy / Utilities / Environment

Westinghouse Electric
Boulevard Paepem, 20
B-1070 Brussels
Tel : (32) (2) 556-8608
Fax :(32) (2) 523-6270
Public Affairs Contact Person: Mr. Odon Duquesne
Title: Regional Manager, Power Systems International
Sector of Activity: Power Generation Equipment

Weyerhaeuser-Weysa
Avenue Louise, 363
B-1050 Brussels
Tel : (32) (2) 648-4345
Fax : (32) (2) 648-8591
Public Affairs Contact Person: Mr. Edmond van Wijnaarden
Title: Managing Director
Public Affairs Contact Person: Mrs. Diane Van Herck
Title: Manager
Sector of Activity: Forest Products / Wood / Paper Board / Banking / Financial Services

CHAPTER 16
THE AMERICAN CLUB OF
BRUSSELS (ACB)

The American Club of Brussels (ACB)
c/o Brussels Sheraton Hotel
Place Rogier, 3
B-1210 Brussels
Tel : (32) (2) 203-6361
Fax : (32) (2) 203-2237
Stephen Freidberg, Executive Director
Janine Lewin, Secretariat

The American Club of Brussels offers many activities and opportunities for socializing and making business contacts.

Once a year, the American Club of Brussels and the American Chamber of Commerce in Belgium organize a joint dinner. This event is always extremely popular and attracts many members from both organizations.

PART II
In the United States

CHAPTER 1
EU SOURCES OF INFORMATION
IN THE USA

EU Delegation to the US
2300 M Street NW
Washington DC 20037-1434
Tel : (1) (202) 862-9500
Tel : (1) (202) 862-9501
Tel : (1), (202) 862-9502
Fax : (1) (202) 429-1766
Hugo Paemen, Chief of Delegation
James Currie, Deputy Chief of Delegation
Mohammed Aziz, Counsellor, Development
Lodewyck Briet, Counsellor, Political Affairs
Yves Devellenes, Economist
Peter Beks, Economic and Commercial Questions

Office of Press and Public Affairs
2300 M Street NW
Washington DC 20037-1434
Tel : (1) (202) 862-9500
Fax : (1) (202) 429-1766
Internet : http://www.eurunion.org

EU Delegation to the United Nations
Dag Hammarksjöld Plaza 3
303 East 47th Street
New York, NY 10017
Tel : (1) (212) 371-3804
Fax : (1) (212) 758-2718
Angel Vinas,Chief of Delegation
Dieter Koenig, Political Affairs
Joseph Cunnane, Economist, Economic & Commercial Questions
Ignacio Garcia Bercero, Economist
Wouter Wilton, Head of Information Service

EU/US Chamber of Commerce
801 Pennsylania Avenue NW - Suite 950
Washington DC 20004
Tel : (1) (202) 347-9292
Fax : (1) (202) 628-5498
Willard M. Berry, President
Christopher Mustain, Manager, Government Relations

European Document Research
1100 17th Street NW - Suite 301
Washington DC 20036
Tel : (1) (202) 785-8594
Fax : (1) (202) 785-8589
Provides a special delivery system of documents relating to specific aspects
of EU Law.Documents may be ordered and received rapidly either by mail or
Fax.

Electronic Information Products Distributors
USA

PSI-USA
4182 Ulysses Way
Golden, Colorado 80403
Tel : (1) (303) 898-4769
Fax : (1) (303) 277-9419

Advanced Information Databases Inc.
P.O. Box 43181
Detroit, MI 48243-0181
Tel : (1) (519) 539-1297
Toll Free : (1) (800) 890-1692
Fax : (1) (519) 539-3176
E-mail : adinfo@adinfo.com
Internet : http://www.adinfo.com
Contact : Allan Bitz
Provides access to EU Databanks

Lexis-Nexis (Host)
9443 Springboro Pike
Dayton, Ohio 45401
Tel : (1) (513) 865-7325
Fax : (1) (513) 865-6949

European Information Services (EIS)
Information Specialist
1452 W; Rascher Avenue # 2
Chicago, IL 60640-1206
Contact: Jésus Bustamente
Tel : (1) (312) 907-8361
Fax : (1) (312)989-8824
E-mail : jesus@tezcat.com

CHAPITRE 2
TEAM EUROPE INFO SERVICE
US LECTURERS FOR EUROPE

Team Europe is a network of 72 Lecturers/Experts in the United States who, upon requests can make presentations on the occasion of Conferences, Seminars, Meetings, etc.

The EU Washington and NY Delegation Offices select Lecturers/Experts based on their extensive knowledge of European Affairs and their competency in sharing their knowledge.

Most often, they are University professors, national or international civil servants, senior executives, consultants, journalists, etc. Members combine an in-depth experience of EU Affairs with a clear understanding of the implications of the various measures, which enable them to adapt to various types of audiences and circumstances.

These Lecturers receive on a regular basis updated information on the most recent developments of Community policies related to their specialization. They also receive the support of a service adapted to their most specific needs, to help them in the elaboration of their Lectures. Fees arrangements are made directly with each Lecturer.

ALPHABETICAL LISTING

Luis Agramunt
Managing Partner
Juris Magister, PA
80 S.W. 8th Street, Suite 2000
Miami, FL 33130
Tel : (1) (305) 373-5802
Fax : (1) (305) 373-5803
Email : iusmundi@aol.com
Topic : EU Law

Dr. Christa Altenstetter
City University of New York
Ph. D. Program in Political Science
33 West 42 Street
New York, NY 10036-8099
Tel : (1) (212) 642-2386
Fax : (1) (212) 642-1980
E-mail : caltenst@gc.cuny.edu
Topic :   Health Insurance
            Health Care
            Social Protection Schemes
            Health Technologies
            Medical Devices Industry

Dr. Nicholas A. Ashford
Professor of Technology and Policy
Massachusetts Institute of Technology
Center for Technology, Policy and Industrial Development
Room E-40-239
Cambridge, MA 02139
Tel : (1) (617) 253-1664
Fax : (1) (617) 253-7140
nashford@mit.edu
Topic : Regulatory Law and Economics

Dr. Carol E. Baumann
Director Emerita,
Institute of World Affairs
University of Wisconsin, Milwaukee
W. 6248 Lake Ellen Drive
Cascade, WI 53011
Tel : (1) (920) 528-8015
Fax : (1) (920) 528-8811
E-mail : cbaumann@excel.net
Topic :   British Attitudes / Policies Towards the EU / History
            Background European Unifications
            US-West European Relations

Dr. George A. Bermann
Professor.
School of Law, Columbia University
435 W. 116th Street, Box A10
New York, NY 10027
Tel : (1) (212) 854-4258
Fax : (1) (212) 854-7946
E -mail : gbermann@lawmail.law.columbia.edu
Topic :   Regulatory Cooperation with EU in Aviation
            Securities
            Food and Drug Regulation

Mr. Robert P. Braubach
Attorney and Counselor at Law
800 Alamo National Building
105 S. St Mary's Street - Suite 800
San Antonio, TX 78205
Tel : (1) (210) 271-8820
Fax: (1) (210) 225-1951
Topic : International Law- EU, US and Mexico

William L. Bryant
Chairman
Bryant Christie, Inc.
1411 Fouth Avenue - Suite 940
Seattle, WA 98101
Tel : (1) (206) 292-6340
Fax: (1) (206) 292-6341
E-mail : bci@bci.iam.com
Topic : Agriculture

Michael Calingaert
Guest Scholar
Brookings Institution
1775 Massachusetts Avenue N.W.
Washington D.C. 20036
Tel : (1) (202) 797-6135
Fax : (1) (202) 797-6133
E-mail : mealingaert@brook.edu
Topic :   European Integration
            Single Market
            US-EU Relations

Dr. Karl Cerny
Professor, Georgetown University
1524 Crestwood Lane
Mc Lean, VA 22101
Tel : (1) (703) 237-2191
Fax : (1) (703) 534-4150
E-mail : cernykh@aol.com
Topic :   Institutional Structure of the Communities and the Decision-Making
           Process : Common Foreign and Security Policy

Dr. J. Bryan Collester
Director, School of Government
Principia College
Department of Political Science
Elsah, IL 62028-9799
Tel : (1) (618) 374-5233
Fax : (1) (618) 374-5122
E-mail : jercol@prin.edu
Topic :   European Integration
           European Security Policy
           Politics of Western Europe

Dr. Stephen Cooney
Manager, International Political Economy. & Policy Development
Siemens Corporation
701 Pennsylvania Avenue NW , Suite 720
Washington D.C. 20004
Tel : (1) (202) 434-4807
Fax: (1) (202) 347-4015
Topic : US-EU Economic Relations

Dr. Wolfgang Danspeckgruber
Executive Director
Center for International Studies
Princeton University
Woodrow Wilson School of Public & International Affairs
Princeton, NJ 08544-1013
Tel : (1) (609) 258-5685
Fax : (1) (609) 258-5349
E-mail : wfd@wws.princeton.edu
Topic : European Foreign and Security Policy

Martha Darling
Senior Manager, Program Management
Boeing Company Airplane Group
c/o 5100 North East 55 th Street
Seattle, WA 98105
Tel : (1) (206) 965-6354
Fax : (1) (206) 965-6388
E-mail : martha.a.darling@boeing.com
Topic : US Business Issues

Duane Deyoe
Deyoe Financial Executive Services
1560 Findlay
PO Box 3141
Boulder, CO 80307-3141
Tel : (1) (303) 499-2393
Fax: (1) (303) 554-1240
E-mail : duane.deyeoe@hotmail.com
Topic :   Health Care
             Insurance
             International Politics
             Trade Issues

Dr. Desmond Dinan
Van Boetzelaerlann 6
NL-2242 SW Wassenaar
Tel : (31) (70) 517-7917
Fax : (31) (70) 517-7917
Topic :   EU-US Relations
             EU-Eastern European Relations

Charles H. Dolan
Senior Vice-President
Cassidy & Associates
700 13th Street NW, Suite 400
Washington DC 20005
Tel : (1) (202) 879-0371
Fax : (1) (202) 347-0785
Topic :   European Government Relations
             Business
             European Politics

John A. Erhardt
President & CEO.
Global Business Relations
201 East 42nd Street, Suite 1506
New York, NY 10017
Tel : (1) (212) 983-6762
Fax : (1) (212) 808 0971
E-mail : globaforum@gnn.com
Topic :   International Business, Trade and Investment
            Environment
            Energy
            Health

Penelope S. Farthing
Partner
Patton Boggs LLP
2550 M Street NW
Washington DC 20037
Tel : (1) (202) 457-6313
Fax : (1) (202) 457-6315
Topic :   Impact of the US on a United Europe

Dr. John C. Fletcher
Managing Director.
Delta Control Group
33146 N. Lakeshore Drive
Wildwood, IL 60030
Tel : (1) (847) 223-7967
Fax : (1) (847) 223-7970
E-mail : jfletcdcg@aol.com
Topic :   Financial Management
            Corporate Governance
            Global Competition

Dr. Ellen L. Frost
Senior Fellow
Institute for International Economics
11 Dupont Circle NW
Washington DC 20036-1207
Tel : (1) (202) 328-9000
Fax : (1) (202) 328-5432
http://www.iic.com
Topic : Transatlantic Trade

Stephen Gallagher
Vice-President
Director Economic Research
Société Générale
1221 Avenue of the Americas
New York, NY 10020
Tel : (1) (212) 278-4496
Fax : (1) (212) 278-7435
Topic :   European Monetary Union (EMU)
           Monetary Issues

James N. Gardner
Attorney
Gardner & Gardner
One World Trade Center
121 S.W. Salmon Street, Suite 1400
Portland, OR 97204-2924
Tel : (1) (503) 224-3024
Fax : (1) (503) 224-3407
E-mail : jngard@aol.com
Topic : EU, Government Relations and Lobbying

Dr. Lily Feldman Gardner
Senior Scholar in Residence
Center for German and European Studies - Georgetown University
School of Foreign Service- ICC 501
Washington DC 20057
Tel : (1) (202) 687-5602
Fax : (1) (202) 687-8359
Topic :   International Relations
           EU Relations with US, Middle East and Eastern Europe
           German Issues

Dr. Maurice Garnier
Professor
Indiana University
Department of Sociology
Bloomington, IN 47405
Tel : (1) (812) 855-2479
Fax : (1) (812) 855-0781
E-mail : garnier@indiana.edu
Topic :   Educational Systems
            African Development

Dr. Roy H. Ginsberg
Director
International Affairs Program - Skidmore College
Saratoga Springs, NY 12866
Tel : (1) (518) 580-5245
Fax : (1) (518) 580-5289
E-mail : rginsberg@skidmore.edu
Topic :   International Relations
            Foreign Policy
            EU Politics/Institutions

Charles N. Goldman
Consultant
Mid Atlantic Club of New York City.
380 Lexington Avenue, Suite 1015
New York, NY 10168
Tel : (1) (212) 534-4038
Fax : (1) (212) 534-3291
Topic : International Legal Matters

Dr. Donald Hancock
Director
Vanderbilt University
Center for European Studies
Box 40, Station B
Nashville, TN 37235
Tel : (1) (615) 322-2528
Fax : (1) (615) 322-2305
E-mail : lonestar@usit.net
Topic :   EU Relations with the US,
            European Free Trade Association (EFTA)
            Eastern Europe

Dr. Michael H. Hayes
Professor of Marketing
University of Colorado at Denver
c/o 10170 Xavier Court
Westminster, CO 80030
Tel : (1) (303) 460-8571
Fax : (1) (303) 556-5899
E-mail : mhayes@castle.cudenver.edu
Topic :   Business and Marketing Strategy in the EU
            General EU Topics

C.Randall Henning
Visiting Fellow
Institute for International Economics
11 Dupont Circle, NW, Suite 620
Washington DC 20036
Tel : (1) (202) 328-9000
Fax : (1)(202)328-5432
E-mail : henning@iie.com
E-mail : henning@american.edu
Topic : European Monetary Union (EMU)

Rio Howard
Trade Development Manager
Port of Seattle
Economic and Trade Development
Pier 69
P.O. Box 1209
Seattle, WA 98111
Tel : (1) (206) 728-3318
Fax : (1) (206) 728-3754
E-mail : howard.r@portseattle.org
Topic :   EU Governance
           Trade and Business
           Telecommunications
           France and the EU
           Transportation
           Trade Policy

Dr Leon Hurwitz
Associate Dean
Cleveland State University
College of Arts & Sciences
Euclid Avenue at East 24 th Street
Cleveland, OH 44115
Tel : (1) (216) 687-3660
Fax : (1) (216) 687-9202
E-mail : l.hurwitz@csuohio.edu
Topic :   Mutual Recognition of Diplomas and Professional Qualifications
           Border Controls

Dr. Hugo M. Kaufmann
Director
European Union Studies Center
The City University of New York
Box 555
33 West 42nd Street
New York, NY 10036
Tel : (1) (212) 642-2977
Fax : (1) (212) 642-2979
E-mail : kaufmann@qcvaxa.qc.edu
Topic :   European Integration
             Economic and Monetary Union
             Growth and Employment Issues in the EU
             The Political Economy of Germany
             Widening and Deepening of the EU

Dr. John T.S. Keeler
Director
University of Washington
Center for West European Studies
216 Thompson , Box 353650
Seattle, WA 98195-3650
Tel : (1) (206) 543-1675
Fax :(1) (206) 685-0668
Fax : (1) (206) 685-2146
E-mail : keeler@u.washington.edu
Topic :   EU Institutions and Policymaking
             Common Agricultural Policy
             France and EU

Dr. Steven Koblik
President
Reed College
3203 S.E. Woodstock Blvd
Portland, OR 97202
Tel : (1) (503) 777-7500
Fax : (1) (503) 777-7701
E-mail : steven.koblik@reed.edu
Topic :   20th Century European History
           Special Interest in Politics,
           Political Economy,
           International Relations, and
           Integration

Dr. Erdogan Kumcu
Associate Professor of Marketing
Ball State University
Muncie, IN 47306-0355
Tel : (1) (765) 275-5186
Fax : (1) (765) 285-8024
E-mail : 00eakumcu@bsu.edu
Topic :   History of EU
           EU-US Business and Economic Relations
           Governance of the EU

Dr. Kate Verlin Laatikainen
Assistant Professor
Chatham College
Department of Political Science
Woodland Road
Pittsburgh, PA 15232
Tel : (1) (412) 365-1153
Fax : (1).(412) 365-1505
E-mail : latikainen@chatham.edu
Topic :   EU Politics
           EU Social and Equality Issues
           Scandinavian-EU Relations
           International Relations

Dr.Peter Lang
Professor of Political Science
Duke University
Box 90204
214 Perkins Library
Durham, NC 27708-0204
Tel : (1) (919) 660-4303
Fax : (1) (919) 660-4330
E-mail : plange@acpub.duke.edu
Topic :   The Social Dimension of the 1992 Process
            Integration Process
            Political Institutions

Dr. Carl Lankowski
Research Director
American Institute for Contemporary German Studies
1400 16th Street NW , Suite 420
Washington DC 20036-2217
Tel : (1) (202) 332-0312
Fax : (1) (202) 265-9531
E-mail : clankow@jhunix.hcf.jhu.edu
Topic :   Environment
            Energy
            Germany and the EU
            European Investment Bank (EIB)
            General Institutional Development

Dr. Pierre-Henri Laurent
Professor of European History
Tufts University
East Hall
Medford, MA 02155
Tel : (1) (617) 627-3520
Fax : (1) (617) 627-3479
E-mail : alazzara@facstaff@as
Topic :   History of the EU
            European Integration

Dr. Alain A. Levasseur
Professor of Law
Louisiana State University
Center for Civil Law Studies
 Law Center 371
Baton Rouge, LA 70803-1006
Tel : (1) (504) 388-1126
Fax : (1) (504) 388-3677
E-mail : alevass@unix 1.sncc.lsu.edu
Topic :   Law and Legal Issues
               Institutions
               Fundamental Freedoms

Dr. Leon N.Lindbergh
Professor of Political Science.
University of Wisconsin - Madison
110 North Hall
Madison, WI 53706
Tel : (1) (608) 263-2414
E-mail : llindberg@polisci.wisc.edu
Topic :   EU Institutions and Policy Making
               Capital Movements
               Financial Services
               Economic and Monetary Union

Robert Mathieson
International Trade Consultant
77 Buttonwood Drive
Dix Hills, NY 11746
Tel : (1) (516) 493-0927
Fax : (1) (516) 462-9650
Topic : International Trade Policy

Dr. John R. Mc Intyre
Georgia Institute of Technology
College of Management
Atlanta, GA 30332-0520
Tel : (1) (404) 894-1463
Fax : (1) (404) 894-6625
E-mail : ciber@mgt.gatech.edu
Topic :   International Trade
            Education
            Consulting
            Technology Transfer

Dr. Kathleen R. Mc Namara
Assistant Professor of Politics and International Affairs
Princeton University
Center for International Studies
Bendheim Hall
Princeton, NJ 08544
Tel : (1) (609) 258-5239
Fax : (1).(609).258-3988
E-mail : mcnamara@wws.prineceton.edu
Topic :   European Integration
            European Monetary Union (EMU)

Dr. Leroy Miller
President
International Business Strategies
1311 Moran Court
North Potomac, MD 20878
Tel : (1) (301) 990-8514
Fax : (1) (301) 670-1685
E-mail : leroymiller@msn.com
Topic : Business Implications of European Integration

Dr. Andrew Moravcsik
Associate Professor of Government
Harvard University
Center for European Studies
27 Kirkland Street
Cambridge, MA 02138
Tel : (1) (617) 495-4303 Ext. 205
Fax : (1) (617) 495-8509
E-mail : moravcs@fas.harvard.edu
Topic :   History and Politics of the EU
           Western Aid to Eastern Europe
           Human Rights
           Transatlantic Relations

Dr. Suman Naresh
Professor of Law
Tulane Law School
6801 Freret Street
New Orleans, LA 70119
Tel : (1) (504) 865-5977
Fax : (1) (504) 862-8859
E-mail : snaresh@law.tulane.edu
Topic :   EU Institutions
           Court of Justice
           EU International Trade Policy
           Competition
           Intellectual Property
           Business and Commercial Law Issues

Dr. Larry Neal
Professor of Economics
University of Illinois
Department of Economics
328A David Kinley Hall
1407 West Gregory Drive
Urbana, IL 61801
Tel : (1) (217) 333-4678
Fax : (1) (217) 333-1398
E-mail : l-neal@uiuc.edu
Topic : Economic Development of Contemporary Europe
International Capital Markets
International Immigration

Dr. Mark K. Neville, Jr.
National Director
Trade & Customs Practices
KPMG, Peat Marwick, LLP
345 Park Avenue
New York, NY 10154
Tel : (1) (212) 872-7709
Fax : (1) (212) 872-3311
Topic : International Trade and Investment
Customs Duties and Regulations

Dr. Mark D. Newman
Director
Food Industry and Agribusiness Consulting
Abt Associates , Inc.
4800 Montgomery Lane , Suite 600
Bethesda, MD 20814
Tel : (1) (301) 913-0500
Fax : (1) (301) 652-3618
E-mail : marknewman@abtassoc.com
Topic : Food and Agricultural Policies and Industries
US/EU Trade and Investment

Dr. Gunnar Nielsson
University of Southern California
School of International Relations
Von Kleinsmid Center 315
Los Angeles, CA 90089-043
Tel : (1) (213) 740-2128
Fax : (1) (213) 742-0281
E-mail : nielsson@bcf.usc.edu
Topic :   European International Politics
            International Organizations

Dr. Seamus O'Cleireacain
Columbia University
Institute on Western Europe
420 West 118th Street
New York, NY 10027
Tel : (1) (212) 854-4618
Fax : (1) (212) 866-6526
E-mail : sco4@columbia.edu
Topic :   European Monetary Union
            Trade Policy
            EU-US Relations
            The Intergovernmental Conference

Dr. Stephen Overturf
Whittier College
Department of Economics
Whittier, CA 90608
Tel : (1) (310) 907-4200
Fax: (1) (310) 698-4067
Topic :   Financial and Monetary Questions (particularly EMU)
            Macroeconomic Implications of Integration

Benjamin L. Palumbo
President
Palumbo & Cerrell
1717 K. Street NW , Suite 500
Washington DC 20006
Tel : (1) (202) 466-9000
Fax : (1) (202) 466-9009
Topic :   Business
            US-EU Relations

Dr. Donald J.Puchala
Director
Richarld L. Walker Institute of International Studies
University of South Carolina
Gambrell Hall- Room 437
Columbia, SC 29208
Tel : (1) (803) 777-8180
Fax : (1) (803) 777-9308
E-mail : puchala@garnet.cla.sc.edu
and Compuserve 75031,1450
Topic :   International Relations
                Fiscal Harmonization
                Global Food Interdependence

Dr. Joseph C. Rallo
Dean, College of Business
Ferris State University
119 South Street
Big Rapids, MI 49307-2284
Tel : (1) (616) 592-2422
Fax : (1) (616) 592-3548
E-mail :ralloj@buso20ferris.edu
Topic :   Security Policy and the EU
                International Technology Policy

Peter Rashish
Executive Vice-President
The European Institute
5225 Wisconsin Avenue NW, Suite 200
Washington DC 20015-2014
Tel : (1) (202) 895-1670
Fax : (1) (202) 362-1088
E-mail : prashish@europeaninstitute.org
Topic :   Transatlantic Trade and Investment
                EU Intergovernmental Conference
                EU/NATO/EU Enlargement

Dr. Carolyn Rhodes
Associate Professor
Department of Political Science
Utah State University
0725 University Boulevard
Logan, UT 84332-0725
Tel : (1) (801) 797-1305
Fax : (1) (801) 797-3751
E-mail : crhodes@wpo.hass.usu.edu
Topic : Integration Theory
International Political Economy
US-European Relations
International Trade Policy

Dr. Glenda Rosenthal
Director
Institute on Western Europe
Columbia University
803B International Affairs Building
420 West 118 Street
New York, NY 10027
Tel : (1) (212) 854-5057
Fax : (1) (212) 854-8599
E-mail : ggr1@columbia.edu
Topic : EU Institutions
Social Dimensions
Commission
EU in context of broader European Affairs

Dr. George Ross
1560 Rue de l'Eglise # 1
St. Laurent, Québec H4L 2H8
Canada
Tel : (1) (514) 744-4809
Fax : (1) (514) 744-4809
E-mail : gwross@fas.harvard.edu
Topic : EU Institutions
Social Dimension
Commission
EU in context of broader European Affairs

Ambassador Edward M. Rowell
Lecturer and Trade Promotion Consultant
5414 Newington Road
Bethesda, MD 20816
Tel : (1) (301) 654-8137
Fax : (1) (301) 654-8137
E-mail : edrowell@erols.com
Topic :   US-European Relations
             European Union
             European Security

Edward W. Russell
Senior Vice-President, Government Affairs
Chase Manhattan Bank
270 Park Avenue
New York, NY 10017-2070
Tel : (1) (212) 270-7050
Fax : (1) (212) 270-5158
Topic :   EMU (European Monetary Union)
             Monetary Issues

Dr. Alberta Sbragia
Director
Center for West European Studies
University of Pittsburg
4E23 Forbes Quadrangle
Pittsburgh, PA 15260
Tel : (1) (412) 648-7405
Fax : (1) (412) 648-2199
E-mail : sbragia@pitt.edu
Topic :   Environmental Policies of the EU
             The Evolution of EU Institutions

Dr. Wolfe A. Schmidt
Chairman/CEO
Schmidt Engineering & Equipment Inc.
1905 South Moorland Road
New Berlin, WI 53151-2321
Tel : (1) (414) 784-6066
Fax : (1) (414) 784-6720
E-mail : was@execpc.com
Topic :   US-European Relations
            Foreign and Security Policy
            Economics and Institutional Aspects of Integration

Professor Beverly J. Springer
Professor Emeritus
4720 W. Greenway
Glendale, AZ 85306
Tel : (1) (602) 978-1064
Fax: (1) (602) 978-1064
E-mail : springrb@aol.com
Topic :   European Integration
            Business Environment in Western Europe
            European Labor and Management
            Employee and Woman's Issues

Sven Steinmo
University of Colorado at Boulder
Department of Political Science
Ketchum 106
Campus Box 333
Boulder, CO 80309
Tel : (1) (303) 492-2525
Fax : (1) (303) 492-3934
E-mail : steinmo@colorado.edu
Topic :   General Overview of the EU
            Financial and Taxation Policy
            Political Economic Relations

Anthony Wallace
George Mason University
4001 North Fairfax Drive
Arlington, VA 22203
Tel : (1) (703) 241-8686
Fax : (1) (703) 835-2379
E-mail : awallac1@gmu.edu
Topic :   Government Procurement
            Standards
            Technology Policy
            Trade Policy

Leslie Williams
Attorney
Shaub & Williams
12121 Wilshire Boulevard, suite 205
Los Angeles, CA 90025
Tel : (1) (310) 826-6678
Fax : (1) (310) 826-8042
E-mail : 74577.1544@compuserve.com
Topic : International Business and Investment Transactions

The Baroness Williams of Crosby
The House of Lords
GB-London SW1A
Tel : (44) (171) 219-5850
Fax : (44) (171) 219-2082
UK switchboard : (44) (171) 219-3000
Harvard : (1) (617) 495-8866
E-mail : swilliam @ksg1.harvard.edu
Topic : Intergovernmental Conference

Dr. David Wilfsford
President and Professor
Institute for American Universities
Place de l'Université, 27
F-1365 Aix-en-Provence
Tel : (33) (4) 223-1382
Fax : (33) (4) 221-1138
E-mail : iaupress@univ.aix.fr
Topic : N/A

The U.S. Practical Guide
to the European Union

Dr. Peter Wollitzer
Regional Director
University of California
Education Abroad Program
Hollister Research Center
Santa Barbara, CA 93106
Tel : (1) (805) 893-2918
Fax : (1) (805) 893-2583
E-mail : wollitze@uoeap.ucsb.edu
Topic :   Internationalization of Higher Education
            Academic Exchanges

Dr. Joachim Zekoll
Professor of Law
Tulane University Law School
6379 Freret Street
New Orleans, LA 70118
Tel : (1) (504) 865-5997
Fax : (1) (504) 862-8844
E-mail : jzekoll@law.tulane.edu
Topic :   International Business Transactions
            EC Products Liability Law
            EU Competition Law
            Dispute Resolution

Geographical Breakdown

Wherever you are, there is an EU Expert you may call on. They are located in 27 states of the US, ready to answer your questions.

Arizona
Professor Beverly J. Springer, Glendale

California
Dr. Gunnar Nielsson, Los Angeles
Dr. Stephen Overturf, Whittier
Leslie Williams, Los Angeles
Dr. Peter Wollitzer, Santa Barbara

Colorado
Duane Deyoe, Boulder
Dr. H. Michael Hayes, Westminster
Sven Steinmo, Boulder

District of Columbia
Michael Calingaert, Washington DC
Dr. Stephen Cooney, Washington DC
Charles H. Dolan, Washington DC
Dr. Lily Gardner Feldman, Washington DC
Dr. Carl Lankowski, Washington DC
Penelope S. Farthing, Washington DC
Dr. Ellen L/ Frost, Washington DC
C. Randall Henning, Washington DC
Bejamin L. Palumbo, Washington DC
Peter Rashish, Washington DC

Florida
LuisAgramunt, Miami

Georgia
Dr. John R. Mc Intryre, Atlanta

Illinois
Dr. J. Bryan Collester, Elsah
Dr. John C. Fletcher, Wildwood
Dr. Larry Neal, Urbana

Indiana
Dr. Maurice Garnier, Bloomington
Dr. Erdogan Kumcu, Kumcu Erdogan, Muncie

Louisiana
Dr. Alain A. Levasseur, Baton Rouge
Dr. Suman Naresh, New Orleans
Dr. Joachim Zekoll

Maryland
Dr. Leroy Miller,North Potomac
Dr. Mark D. Newmann, Bethesda
Ambassador Edward M. Rowell, Bethesda

Massachusetts
Dr. Nicholas A. Ashford, Cambridge
Dr. Pierre-Henri Laurent, Medford
Dr. Andrew Moravcsik, Cambridge

Michigan
Dr. Joseph C. Rallo, Big Rapids

New Jersey
Dr. Wolfgang Danspeckgruber, Princeton
Dr. Kathleen R. McNamara, Princeton

New York
Dr. Christa Altenstetter, New York
Dr. George A. Bermann, New York
John A. Erhardt, New York
Stephen Gallagher, New York
Dr. Roy H. Ginsberg, Saratoga Springs
Charles N. Goldman, New York
Dr Hugo M. Kaufmann, New York
Robert Mathieson, Dix Hills
Dr. Mark K. Neville, Jr., New York
Dr. Seamus O'Cleireacain, New York
Dr. Glenda Rosenthal, New York
Edward W. Russell, New York

North Carolina
Dr. Peter Lang, Durham

Ohio
Dr. Leon Hurwitz, Cleveland

Oregon
James N. Gardner, Portland
Dr. Steven Koblik, Portland

Pennsylvania
Dr. Alberta Sbragia, Pittsburgh
Dr. Kate Verlin Laatikainen, Pittsburgh

South Carolina
Dr. Donald J. Puchala, Columbia

Tennessee
Dr. Donald Hancock, Nashville

Texas
Robert P. Braubach, San Antonio

Utah
Dr. Carolyn Rhodes, Logan

Virginia
Dr. Karl Cerny, Mc LeanCerny Karl, Mc Lean
Anthony Wallace, Arlington

Washington
William L. Bryant, Seattle
Martha Darling, Seattle
Rio Howard, Seattle
Dr. John T.S. Keeler, Seattle

Wisconsin
Dr. Carol E. Baumann, Cascade
Dr. Leon N. Lindbergh, MadisonLindbergh Leon N., Madison
Dr. Wolfe A. Schmidt, New Berlin

Canada
Dr. George Ross, St. Laurent, Quebec

France
Dr. David Wilsford, Aix-en-Provence

Netherlands
Dr. Desmond Dinan, Wassenaar

United Kingdom
The Baroness Williams of Crosby

CHAPTER 3
EU INFORMATION CENTERS IN THE USA

The US Libraries listed hereafter receive automatically from the Commission all EU publications. They also have access to the Community's database. In some instances, and depending on the specialization of the teachers, they may only request information on specific sectors of activity.

State University of New York at Albany
University Library
Western Avenue 1223
Albany, NY, 12203

The University of New Mexico
Zimmerman Library - Gift and Exchange Section
Albuquerque, NM 87131
Professor/Director: D. L. Papstein
Librarian/Assistant: D. L. Papstein

University of Michigan
Law Library - Serials Department
Ann Arbor, MI 48109
Professor/Director: B. J. Pooley
Librarian/Assistant: Mrs R. Maripuu

George Mason University
Center for European Community Studies
Arlington Campus
4001 N. Fairfax Dr. Suite 450
Arlington, VA 22203
Tel : (1) (703) 993 8200
Fax : (1) (703) 993 8215
Professor/Director: D. Dinan
Librarian/Assistant: Miss C. Hurt

University of Georgia
School of Law - Law Library
Athens, GA 30602
Tel : (1) (706) 542-1922
Fax : (1) (706) 542-5001
Professor/Director: G. M. Wilner
Librarian/Assistant: J. Pages

Emory University
Atlanta State of Georgia
Government Documents
Gambell Hall
Atlanta, GA 30322
Tel : (1) (404) 727-6796
Fax : (1) (404) 727-6820
Professor/Director: R. Mills
Librarian/Assistant: Mrs C. Wang

University of Texas at Austin
School of Law Library
727 East 26th Street
Austin, TX 78705
Professor/Director: R. M. Mersky
Librarian/Assistant: R. M. Mersky

University of California
Government Documents Department
General Library
Berkeley, CA 94720
Librarian/Assistant: G. Nichols

Indiana University
Library - Documents Department
Bloomington, IN 47405
Tel : (1) (812) 855-6924
Fax : (1) (812) 855-3460
Librarian/Assistant: A. Wichizer

University of Colorado at Boulder - Library
Government Publications Division
Box 184
Boulder, CO 80309
Professor/Director: Mrs Lee Carter

State University of New York at Buffalo
Serials Department - European Communities
Central Technic. Serv.
Loockwood Library Building
Buffalo, NY 14260
Librarian/Assistant: F. K. Henrich

Harvard Law School Library
Collection Development Department
Langdell Hall, LW 431
Cambridge, MA 02138
Tel : (1) (617) 495-3172
Fax : (1) (617) 495-4449

University of Illinois
Law Library
East Pennsylvania Avenue, 504
Champaign, IL 61820
Tel : (1) (617) 333-2913
Fax : (1) (617) 244-8500
Professor/Director: F. Mansfield

University of Virginia
The Alderman Library - Government Documents
Charlottesville, VA 22903-2498
Tel : (1) (804) 924-3133
Fax : (1) (804) 924-4337
Librarian/Assistant: B. M. Smith

University of Chicago
Joseph Regenstein Library
Documents Department
2425 East 57th Street
Chicago, IL 60637-1502
Librarian/Assistant: M. L. Walters

Library of International Relations
Chicago College of Law
West Adams Street 565
8th Floor
Chicago IL 60611-3691
Tel : (1) (312) 906-5622
Fax : (1) (312) 906-5685
Librarian/Assistant: Ms J. Statham

University of Iowa
Libraries - Continuation Acquisition Division
Columbus OH 43210
Librarian/Assistant: B. A. Black

University of South Carolina
Thomas Cooper Library
Documents - Microforms
Columbia, S.C. 29208
Professor/Director: L. E. Duncan Jr
Librarian/Assistant: L. E. Duncan Jr

Duke University
Perkins Library
Public Documents and Maps Department
Box 90117
Durham, NC 27708
Tel : (1) (919) 684-2380
Fax : (1) (919) 684-2855
Librarian/Assistant: L. Williams

Michigan State University
Documents Department - Library
East Lansing, MI 48824
Librarian/Assistant: D. Brunn

University of Oregon
Documents Section - The Library
Eugene, OR 97403
Tel : (1) (503) 34630 - 90
Librarian/Assistant: T. A. Stave

Texas Christian University
Mary Courts Burnett Library
Box 32904
Fort Worth, TX 72129
Tel : (1) (817) 921-7106
Fax : (1) (817) 921-7110
Professor/Director: J. Newcomer

Northwestern University
The University Library
Government Publications Department
Evanston, IL 60208-2300
Tel : (1) (708) 491-3130
Fax : (1) (708) 491-5685

University of Florida
Smathers Libraries
Documents Department Library Unit
Gainesville, FL 32611
Tel : (1) (904) 392-0366
Fax : (1) 904) 392-7251
Librarian/Assistant: S. Cravens

University of Hawaii Library
Government Documents Collection
Campus Road 2425
Honolulu, HI 96822
Librarian/Assistant: E. C. Au

University of California - San Diego
Serials Acquisitions - Acquisitions Department Library 0175
Gilmon Drive 9500
Department 0175 P
La Jolla - CA 92093
Librarian/Assistant: P. Zarins

University of Kansas
Government Documents and Map Library
Malott Hall 6001
Lawrence, KS 66045
Tel : (1) (913) 864-4660
Professor/Director: A. K. Head
Librarian/Assistant: W. Cardillo

University of Kentucky
Central Serials Record
Lexington, KY 40506 - 0039
Librarian/Assistant: J. Pivarnik

University of Nebraska - Lincoln
The University Library
Acquisitions Department
Lincoln, NE 68588
Professor/Director: R. Zariski
Librarian/Assistant: T. L. Yien

University of Arkansas - ULAR
Documents Department - ULAR Library
2801 South University Avenue
Little Rock, ARK. 72204
Tel : (1) (501) 569-8806
Fax : (1) (501) 569-3017
Librarian/Assistant: S. Wold

University of California
Public Affairs Service/International
University Research Library
405 Hilgard Avenue
Los Angeles, CA 90024
Librarian/Assistant: B. Silvernail

University of Southern California
Doheny Memorial Library
University Park - MC 0182
Los Angeles CA 90089
Librarian/Assistant: S. Stern

University of Wisconsin
Serials Department - Memorial Library
728 State Street
Madison, WI 53706
Professor/Director: V. Hill
Librarian/Assistant: R. Sanderson

University of Minnesota
Government Publications - Library Department
Wilson Library 409
19th Avenue South 309
Minneapolis, MN 55455
Tel : (1) (612) 624-0241
Librarian/Assistant: W. La Bissoniere

Yale University
Government Documents Center - Seeley G. Mudd Library
38 Mansfield Street
P. O. Box 208294
New Haven, CT 06520
Tel : (1) (203) 432-3209
Fax : (1) (203) 432-3214
Librarian/Assistant: M. Sullivan

University of New Orleans
Earl K. Long Library
Serials Department
Lakefront
New Orleans, LA 70148
Tel : (1) (504) 286-7276
Fax : (1) (504) 286-7277
Professor/Director: Mrs S. Boudreaux
Librarian/Assistant: Mrs M. Hankel

New York Public Library
Division E
Grand Central Station
P. O. Box 2221
New York, NY 10017
Librarian/Assistant: Miss E. F. Beder

New York University
School of Law Library
40, Washington Square South
New York, NY 10012
Librarian/Assistant: J. J. Marke

The Harold Pratt House
Council on Foreign Relations Inc.
Library
58 East 68th Street
New York, NY 10021

University of Oklahoma
Government Documents Collection
Bizzell Memorial Library, Room 440
401 West Brooks
Norman, OK 73019
Tel : (1) (405) 325-2611
Librarian/Assistant: J. K. Zink

University of Notre Dame
Memorial Library - Document Center
Notre Dame, IND 46556
Professor/Director: Mr Francis
Librarian/Assistant: T. B. Ivanus

University of Maine
Raymond H. Fogler Library
Orono, ME 04473
Librarian/Assistant: J. C. Mc Campbell

University of Pennsylvania
Van Pelt Dietrich Library - Serials Department
3420 Walnut Street
Philadelphia, 4 PA 19104-6278
Tel : (1) (215) 898-7555
Fax : (1) (215) 898-0559
Librarian/Assistant: M. A. Crozer

University of Pittsburgh
Hilman Library G - 72 Gift and Exchange
Pittsburgh, PA 15260
Librarian/Assistant: C. Vana

University of Maine
Law Library
Deering Avenue 246
Portland, ME 04102

Princeton University
Library - Documents Division
One Washington Road
Princeton, NJ 08544
Tel : (1) (609) 258-3178
Librarian/Assistant: Mrs S. Burkman

Mariott Library
International Documents Section
Documents Division - University of Utah
Salt Lake City, UT 84112
Tel : (1) (801) 581-8394
Fax : (1) (801) 581-4882
Librarian/Assistant: J. Hinz

University of Washington
Libraries FM - 25
Government Publications Section
Seattle, WA 98195
Librarian/Assistant: E. L. Chase

Hoover Institution
Central & Western European Collections
Serials Department
Stanford, CA 94305-1687
Tel : (1) (415) 725-3595
Fax : (1) (415) 723-1687
Librarian/Assistant: A. F. Peterson

Washington University
Libraries/Serials Unit
Lindell & Skinker Blvds
St Louis, MO 63130
Librarian/Assistant: R. Rotkowicz

University of Arizona
University Library
Tucson, AR 85721
Professor/Director: J. P. Schaefer
Librarian/Assistant: D. Laird

Pennsylvania State University
Libraries - Documents Section
University Park, PA 16802
Librarian/Assistant: S. A. Anthes

Center for Research and Documentation on the European Community
(C.E.R.D.E.C.)
The American University
305 Bender Library
Nebraska & Massachusetts Avenues, NW
Washington DC 20016
Professor/Director: M. Struelens
Librarian/Assistant: G. Somera

Library of Congress
Exchange and Gift Division
(IGO - EUDOM)
10 First Street S.E.
Washington DC 20540

ANNEX A
THE ECONOMIC RELATIONSHIP

Transatlantic economic relations are underpinned by the most important trade and investment links in the world. Such links have grown particularly strongly over the last few years, to the benefit of both economies. Meanwhile, the two sides remain each other's most important source and destination for foreign direct investment.

TRADE IN GOODS

Trade in goods (exports and imports) between the European Union (excluding the three new Member States i.e. Austria, Finland and Sweden) and the US reached nearly 190 billion ECU in 1994, an increase of about 11% over the previous year. After the EU registered a trade deficit with the US for three consecutive years from 1990 to 1992, in 1993 and 1994 bilateral trade was almost in equilibrium (surplus of 0.6 billion ECU and 2.5 billion ECU respectively). Complete EU data for 1995 are not yet available, but EU (12) data for the first 9 months indicate a, slight EU deficit of about 3.3 billion ECU in the bilateral trade balance.

The US is the EU's single largest trading partner, accounting for 17% to 18% in both total EU imports and total EU exports in 1994. Likewise, the EU is one of the two top markets for the US accounting for 21% of US exports and 18% of US imports in 1994.

The EU and the US are the world's most important traders. The share of the EU in total world trade (excluding intra-EU trade) amounted to 20% in 1994; while the share of the US amounted to 18.3%. Taking only bilateral EU-US trade, it represents almost 7% of total world trade. This was only marginally less compared to US-Canada trade which was 7.4%. Trade between US and Japan represented 5.5% of total world trade.

TRADE IN SERVICES

Transatlantic trade in services is gaining importance both in absolute terms and relative to merchandise trade. In 1988, EU-US trade in services accounted for 71.4 billion ECU or about 51% of trade in goods. By 1993, this figure had risen to 114.1 billion ECU or approximately 67% of merchandise trade.

INVESTMENT FLOWS

The EU and US have by far the world's most important bilateral investment relationship, and each is the other's largest investment partner. In 1993, which is the most recent year for which EU data is available, the strong, mutual links between the US and the EU were confirmed with the EU investing 10.2 billion ECU (accounting for 47% of the total EU outward Foreign Direct Investment, FDI) in the US and the US investing 9 billion ECU in the EU (accounting for 43% of the total EU inward FDI).

The cumulated flows over the period 1984-1993 shows that the US was the single largest contributor with 33% of the EU inflows. Conversely, in the same period almost 60% of EU investment abroad went to the US. The US is thus the most important source and destination of EU DFI).

Source : Eurostat-Comext Database

ANNEX B
THE NEW TRANSATLANTIC AGENDA

The New Transatlantic Agenda marks a major step forward in strengthening relations between the EU and the US.

The framework for action is designed to translate common political and economic objectives into practical measures centered around four major priorities:

1. Promoting peace and stability, democracy and development around the world. This priority covers support for the peace process in various regions of the world, particularly the former Yugoslavia and the Middle East, development cooperation, humanitarian aid, promotion of human rights and democracy, nuclear non-proliferation and cooperation in international organizations.

2. Responding to global challenges, particularly the fight against international crime, terrorism and drug trafficking, protecting the environment and public health.

3. Contributing to the expansion of world trade and closer economic relations by strengthening the multilateral trading system and eliminating barriers to transatlantic trade.

4. Building bridges across the Atlantic by developing links between business circles, scientists and universities on both sides of the Atlantic and by encouraging cultural cooperation.

Implementation of these priorities will be monitored and if necessary they will be updated at the six monthly presidential level meetings.

ANNEX C
UNITED STATES BARRIERS TO
TRADE AND INVESTMENT
AS REPORTED BY THE EU COMMISSION

Report compiled by the Unit for Relations with the United States of America of the Directorate General for External Relations: Commercial Policy and Relations with North America, the Far East, Australia and New Zealand on the basis of material available to the services of the European Commission. The purpose of this report is to provide an inventory of obstacles that European exporters and investors enounter in the US.

Within the framework of the New Transatlantic Agenda (NTA) both the EU and the US are committed, not only to strengthen and consolidate the multilateral trading system, but also to create a New Transatlantic Marketplace, by progressively reducing or eliminating barriers that hinder the flow of goods, services and capital between the EU and the US. As part of this latter initiative there will be a joint EU-US study on ways of facilitating trade and reducing or eliminating such barriers.

This Report also has to be seen in the context of a Transatlantic economic relationship which has grown particularly strongly over the years to the benefit of both economies, and which is underpinned by the most important trade and investment links in the world.

The fact remains, however, that a considerable number of impediments, ranging from more traditional tariff and non-tariff barriers, to differences in the legal and regulatory systems, or due to the absence of internationally agreed rules and disciplines in new areas such as investment and competition policy, still need to be tackled. The Commission remains firmly committed to adressing these through the appropriate channels (multilateral, plurilateral and bilateral) in particular since the reinforcement of efforts to resolve bilateral trade issues and disputes is essential to the confidence building process which is an integral part of the New Transtlantic Agenda.

EXTRATERRITORIALITY

The European Union opposes the extraterritorial provisions of certain US legislation which hamper international trade and investment by seeking to regulate EU trade with third countries conducted by companies outside the United States. Particular problems are raised at the present time with regard to US legislative initiatives concerning Cuba, Iran, and Libya.

UNILATERALISM

Unilateralism in US trade legislation is a major concern. The use of such legislation undermines the internationally-agreed system of trade rules embodied in the World Trade Organization. (WTO) This is true than ever following the extension of WTO disciplines to new fields such as services and intellectual property.

NATIONAL SECURITY

Although the principle of national security has a long tradition in trade policy, the EU has repeatedly expressed concern about its excessive use by the United States as a disguised form of protectionism, particularly in relation to the application of import, procurement and investment restrictions, as well as the extraterritorial application of export restrictions.

PUBLIC PROCUREMENT

Even before the Uruguay Round had been ratified, the EU and US had concluded negotiations on further bilateral procurement agreement that improves on the provisions of the WTO Government Procurement Agreement. These two agreements increase substantially the bidding opportunities for the two sides. However, the EU remains concerned about the wide variety of «Buy America » provisions which persist, and to which are being added others for federally funded infrastructure programs.

TARIFF BARRIERS

Tariffs have been substantially reduced in successive GATT rounds. As a result, the EU's concern is focused on a relatively limited number of US « peak » tariffs, where less progress has been made. Beyond this, EU exports also face a number of additional customs impediments, which add to cost in a similar way to tariffs such as the Merchandising Processing Fee and the excessive invoicing requirements on importers. The EU is working with the US to try to alleviate some of these difficulties.

TECHNICAL BARRIERS TO TRADE

EU exporters continue to face a number of behind- the- border impediments. The proliferation of regulation at State level presents particular problems for companies without offices in the United States. In addition, some federal standards differ from international norms meaning that manufacturers cannot directly export to the US products made to EU standards (normally based on international ones). Other related difficulties concern labelling requirements and excessive reliance on third-party certification. Finally, the FDA drug approval procedures continue to give non-US based firms difficulties.

INTELLECTUAL PROPERTY

As with other sectors, the implementation of Uruguay Round commitments are changing the legislative landscape for intellectual property rights. Although recent changes to patent law are welcome, some problems remain including that of informing right-holders of government use of patents.

TAX MEASURES

Concern about federal tax measures focus on the nature of reporting requirements and the specific manner for calculating what is due. More significantly, however, State « world-wide » unitary taxes are inconsistent with US obligations under its tax treaties with third countries.

CONDITIONAL NATIONAL TREATMENT

Although the present Congress does not appear to be threatening the same kind of widespread restrictions on national treatment as its predecessor, the EU is eager to work with the US to establish solid ground rules for the national treatment of investors, so as to provide a framework which gives business real confidence when they invest abroad

AGRICULTURE AND FISHERIES

The conclusion of the Uruguay Round has to some extent given rise to an easing of trade tensions in agriculture but a variety of issues remain unresolved and some others have re-emerged. Certainly, US export subsidies should become less of a concern over the course of the six year Uruguay Round transition period. Sanitary and phytosanitary issues have therefore become the main source of difficulty for the EU. There is also concern about the abuse of geographic designations for wines.

Little progress in the fisheries sector can be reported. EU concerns focus on US unilateral determinations concerning other countries' fishing practices.

SHIPBUILDING

The conclusion in the OECD of a Shipbuilding Agreement in December 1994 is anticipated to go a long way towards regulating unfair practices in this industry. While the EU expects the US will ratify the Agreement soon, it remains concerned about a number of US subsidies and tax policies.

AERONAUTICS INDUSTRY

The EU remains concerned about the level of implicit subsidies to US aircraft manufacturers. This is clearly an area for multilateral action, and progress needs to be made on Civil Aircraft which remains stalled in the WTO.

MARITIME SERVICES

With the entry into force of the WTO GATS disciplines, this sector is for the first time subject to multilateral trade rules. Although there are no specific commitments as yet to reduce trade barriers the EU remains hopeful that the ongoing negotiations in the WTO context will be brought to a successful completion by the agreed deadline. The US reluctance to table an offer so far is a matter of concern.

In addition, there has been no progress on the elimination of requirements that cargoes generated by US Federal programs be shipped on US-flagged ships, on the contrary, this requirement has been extended to cover Alaskan oil exports.

TELECOMMUNICATIONS SERVICES

The European Commission is fully committed to achieving an effective implementation of the World Trade Organization (WTO) agreement on basic telecommunications services, both within and outside the European Union. The Commission welcomes the inclusion of the implementation of this agreement in the Transatlantic Business Dialogue (TABD) agenda, with a view to identify problems, and to propose solutions.

AUTOMOTIVE SECTOR

The European Commission is fully engaged in the process of international harmonization of automotive regulations, undertaken in the framework of the United Nations Economic Commission in Europe. (UN/ECE) both under the existing Revised 1958 Agreement (to which the Commission will adhere as soon as the European Parliament has given its assent) as well as under the so-called Parallel Agreement which is currently under negotiation in Geneva. The Commission welcomes the efforts which EU and US industries are making in the context of the TABD towards international harmonization.

Regarding Tyres, the Commission welcomes the efforts being made by the EU and US industries to prepare the way for further international harmonization of tyre regulations-including mutual recognition of tests and certification- in the framework of the UN/ECE

PHARMACEUTICALS

The Commission supports industry's call for a transatlantic pharmaceutical marketplace that encourages research and discovery of innovative medicines; in particular, it seeks more pricing freedom and the curtailing of parallel trade in Europe, the repeal of the Bolar amendment in the United States, and the introduction of a uniform 10-year term for data protection on both sides of the Atlantic.

CHEMICALS

The European Commission supports efforts to simplify the notifications procedures for new polymers and low-risk chemicals in 1998. It also welcomes the proposal for a Memorandum of Understanding on good laboratory practice (GLP)

BIOTECHNOLOGY

The Commission supports the principle of transparent and predictable regulatory processes for biotechnology-derived agro-food products-what industry terms the "once approved, accepted everywhere" in the transatlantic marketplace Industry's system. However, in the Commission view, safety must take precedence over speed, particularly in an issue where consumer confidence is so important. The Commission supports industry's suggestion of a system of mutual recognition of data as the basis for better mutual understanding of procedures for putting such products on the market.

AIR TRANSPORT

Progress need to be made on the issues of computer reservation systems and foreign ownership restrictions. The Commission is also concerned with the Hatch amendment which it views as a breach of international rules.

FINANCIAL SERVICES

The US financial services industry is in the throes of major reform, which will sweep away many of the inter-state banking restrictions to the benefit of US and non US banks as well as their customers. However, US sectoral segmentation rules remain in place and effectively block the establishment of globally integrated financial services organizations. This has consequences for EU firms making strategic business decisions for the single European market. For example, link ups between banks and insurance firms face difficulties if both parties have US subsidiaries

As regards activity in the WTO, the US decision only to make partial commitments in the context of the extended GATS negotiations- and to take broad MFN exemptions in respect of future business and activities-reduces the value of the liberalization package secured in these negotiations.

PROFESSIONAL SERVICES

The implementation of the GATS schedules for professional services should result in some improvement in market access. However, a number of problems, especially due to regulation at the State level, still remain to be tackled in order to secure a more transparent and open access to the US.

INFORMATION SOCIETY

The European Union is moving rapidly towards a largely deregulated market without ownership restrictions, and is looking to the on-going-and recently prolonged-GATS Basic Telecommunications negotiations to engage all the leading industrialized parties in a firm set of commitments on market access respecting the MFN principle and national treatment.

The EU remains concerned about the considerable hurdles that the US legislation presents for non-US firms and foreign-owned firms wishing to invest in radio telecommunications infrastructure and to provide mobile and satellite services. In addition, the Federal Communications Commission (FCC) exercises a high degree of autonomy and discretion in regulating this sector, including reciprocity-based licensing procedures for foreign-owned firms.

IMPACT OF THE NEW TRANSATLANTIC AGENDA

The New Transatlantic Agenda (NTA) commits the EU and the US to the creating of a « New Transatlantic Marketplace » by progressively reducing, or eliminating barriers that hinder the flow of goods, services and capital across the Atlantic. There is also a commitment to fostering an active and vibrant transatlantic community by deepening and broadening commercial, social, cultural, scientific and educational ties. Specific initiatives that are of particular relevance are :

- The negotiation of a Mutual Recognition Agreement covering various sectors. This will allow certification to US standards by EU bodies, and vice versa, thus eliminating some of the considerable costs involved for manufacturers on either side of the Atlantic.
- Regulatory cooperation seeking to make regulators more aware of the trade and investment consequences of their decisions and to discourage the development of divergent regulations. The existing dialogues between regulators should play a more substantial role in addressing issues which might otherwise become the source of a future trade dispute.
- The negotiation of a customs cooperation and mutual assistance agreement which will cover simplification of customs procedures, data and personnel exchanges and increased investigative cooperation.
- The launching of negotiations for a science and technology agreemen with a view to broadening cooperation in this field.

INDEX